SEMPER and SCORE

Enhancing enterprise effectiveness

Tom Graves

Tetradian Consulting

Published by
Tetradian Books
Unit 215, Communications House
9 St Johns Street, Colchester CO2 7NN
England

www.tetradian.com
www.sempermetrics.com

First published: July 2008
ISBN 978-1-906681-10-4 (paperback)
ISBN 978-1-906681-11-1 (e-book)

Contents

Acknowledgements

The author would like to acknowledge the assistance of Elizabeth Hagiefremidis, Holly Dinh, Marcus Barber, Norm Currie, Jan Wild and others in the SD / SLaM group in Melbourne, in reviewing and testing the early versions of the SEMPER diagnostic and Five Element techniques. In particular, Holly Dinh provided the key concept of 'word pictures' for scoring, as used in SEMPER-5. Thanks are also due to David Holmes, Graeme Burnett and others for allowing me to apply and validate the initial ideas for the Five Elements framework within business-critical issues in engineering support.

Amongst others, the following people kindly provided comments and feedback on the early drafts of this book: Sally Bean (London, GB); Shawn Callahan (Anecdote, Aus), Valerie Graves (Colchester, GB), Jamie Milne (Smart421, GB), Elizabeth Poraj-Wilczynska (Brockhampton, GB), Dave Snowden (Cognitive Edge, SG), Peter Tseglakof (AusPost, Aus).

Please note that, to preserve commercial and personal confidentiality, the stories and examples have been adapted, combined and in part fictionalised from experiences in a variety of contexts, and do not and are not intended to represent any specific person or organisation.

INTRODUCTION

Enhancing enterprise effectiveness

All organisations strive for high performance, in the short-term at least. Yet the real 'holy grail' is *sustainable excellence* – even in fast-changing times.

The usual recommendation for this is an almost obsessive focus on efficiency above everything else. True, an emphasis on efficiency will help in some ways; but the only way to sustain excellence in the long term is through focusing on *effectiveness* – of which efficiency is only one part. Effectiveness in turn depends on integration, on understanding and working with the enterprise *as a whole*. How to do so is what this book describes.

As explained in previous books in this series – such as *Real Enterprise Architecture: beyond IT to the whole enterprise* (or 'Real EA') – developing and maintaining a clear picture of the whole is a key task for the enterprise-architect. Yet this book will also be useful for anyone whose work addresses or encompasses the whole enterprise – senior strategists and analysts, executives and senior management, Programme Management Office and similar roles. And the concepts and techniques described here can be used in any kind of enterprise, at every scale, from a single-person project to a large multi-national corporation or even an entire country.

Themes we'll address here include:

- what is enterprise effectiveness?
- what impact does effectiveness have on enterprise performance?
- what impact does strategy have on enterprise effectiveness?
- how can we measure and monitor effectiveness?
- how can we use those metrics to enhance overall effectiveness?

In other words, a bit of theory to set the context, but the remainder is very much a practical 'how-to' – a cook-book that's seasoned with real-world examples. But first, a simple question with a not-so-simple answer:

What is effectiveness?

What *is* 'effectiveness', in an enterprise sense? The usual management texts seem to imply either that effectiveness is the same as efficiency, or else assert that we need to be "efficient and effective" without actually describing what is meant by 'effective' or how it differs from efficiency. In other words, 'effective' is, well, *effective* an' all that, y'know? Which isn't much help... To enhance enterprise effectiveness, we need something that's a lot more concrete than that kind of vague, woolly non-definition.

So let's be explicit: effectiveness consists of, or arises from, four distinct dimensions, plus another sort-of dimension that ties the others together:

- *efficient* – makes the best use of available resources
- *reliable* – can be relied on to deliver the required results
- *elegant* - supports the human factors in the context
- *appropriate* – supports and sustains the overall purpose
- *integrated* - linked to and supports integration of the whole *as* whole

Enterprise performance depends on how well we optimise across these dimensions, and the set of related dimensions that, between them, express the enterprise's 'ability to do work'. More detail on that in the next chapter; the point here is that efficiency is neither the same as effectiveness, nor separate from it, but a *subset* of what's needed for overall effectiveness.

The danger, then, is that a focus on efficiency alone will almost always cause more harm than good, because we cannot optimise appropriately against the other dimensions of effectiveness. Yet many, perhaps most, of the standard management texts still promote the assumption that efficiency is the be-all-and-end-all of business: what's going on? The short answer is that they're using the wrong metaphor to describe the enterprise – which at first might sound somewhat abstract, but the impacts on enterprise capability and performance are all too real. To understand *why* it's such a problem, and what to do about it, it's worthwhile taking a brief detour to look at this matter of metaphor.

A matter of metaphor

For more than a century, the most common metaphor to describe the enterprise is to think of it as a *machine* – more specifically, in the commercial context, as 'a machine for making money' on behalf of the shareholders. This is the core concept behind 'scientific management', of 'business process re-engineering' and so many other theories and models of the enterprise. In my main field of enterprise-architecture, for example, it's the basis for John Zachman's oft-repeated assertion that the role of architecture is 'engineering the enterprise'. And so on, and so on.

It's been around so long, and been dominant for so long, that it doesn't seem like a metaphor at all: it's *the* description of how things really *are*. But despite that sense of certainty, of 'naturalness', in reality it's just one of many possible metaphors, and by no means the best – in fact, for most present-day enterprises, it's dangerously misleading. For practical purposes, it's far better to think of the enterprise as a *living organism*. The contrast between these two metaphors is striking:

Machine	Living organism
Purpose provided from outside (has no inherent purpose)	Purposive, self-motivating
Requires outside agency to adapt for change or repair	Self-adapting, self-repairing
Rule-based: cannot cope with complexity	Can handle full spectrum of rules, guidelines, heuristics, principles
Sum of its parts	May be more (or less) than sum of its parts
Can be taken apart and rebuilt	Likely to fail ('die') if taken apart

Metaphors: machine versus living organism

If we view the enterprise as a machine, then our only concerns are efficiency and reliability – hence 'scientific management', and its obsession with control. From this perspective, it's 'obvious' that people are 'human resources', interchangeable components to be linked into the functions of the machine via standardised job-descriptions. It's equally 'obvious' that, wherever practicable, people should be replaced by software, because (in theory at least) machines are more predictable than people – hence the delusory allure of theories such as business process re-engineering…

Business process re-engineering has been described as "the last gasp of Taylorism" – the final act of hubris that highlighted all the fundamental flaws in 'scientific management'. I've yet to hear of *any* BPR project that delivered all its promised benefits: instead, most cases came close to destroying the entire enterprise.

Some years after the initial exuberant hype, and when the true scale of the debacle had become too much to ignore, one of BPR's most ardent proponents ruefully admitted that "we failed to take enough account of the human factors". Hmm... methinks 'failed to take *any* account of the human factors' might have been more accurate...

For all its appeal, its apparent simplicity, the machine metaphor has some lethal limitations. For example, it assumes a strict separation between 'brawn' and 'brain' – the classic distinction between 'blue-collar' versus 'white-collar'. And the real thinking for how to reconfigure and restructure the machine must always come from outside – hence lucrative employment for armies of self-styled 'management consultants'. Yet the catch in doing so is that the 'brain' is distanced from the action, hence keeping track of what's going is always uncertain; communication takes too much time; decisions are always too late; and key details are often lost or misinterpreted, causing decisions to be flawed at best. When the wrong information and other resources arrive in the wrong place, with the wrong person, at the wrong time or in the wrong sequence, life can be hell out there on the factory floor...

So whilst the machine metaphor is efficient in theory, it's often appallingly ineffective in practice. (In fact it fails *because* the focus is theory, not practice – though more on that later.) The only business-contexts for which it *does* work well are those with stable, slow-changing markets and simple, highly standardised products or services – which applies to very few enterprises in the present-day. The machine metaphor simply cannot cope with the current global trends, such as growing diversity and division; the need for differentiation in a globalised, commodified market; increasing value of information; outsourcing and other 'extended enterprise' relationships; emerging networks, 'value webs', and other dynamic consortia; 24/7 'follow-the-sun' business-processes, and the ever-increasing pace and complexity of change.

No doubt, of course, that every enterprise will still need continuous improvements in efficiency, to cope with the relentless pressure to do more with less; and every business system and business process will still need reliability, wherever we can find it. Yet most real-world enterprises *also* need a model that allows for uncertainty and unpredictability, for complexity and rapid change. Which is where the metaphor of the 'living enterprise' comes into the picture.

In a living organism, the 'brain' isn't separate from the 'brawn': each is part of and dependent on the other. A large enterprise, just like a large organism, is a complex web of interdependent specialised services woven into a single 'viable system'; and as systems-theory pioneer Stafford Beer put it, the real 'brain of the firm' does not reside solely with the managers, but is distributed throughout the enterprise. The same is true of the enterprise's knowledge of itself and its environment – the key concerns of enterprise-architecture; these arise from the 'human factors', from personal skills, personal knowledge, relationships, purpose, commitment, drive. Such things have no meaning to a machine – but they matter a great deal to a living enterprise.

Without access to that 'distributed brain', the enterprise is likely to be in deep trouble in today's complex environment; but when that knowledge and awareness and creativity are available, and shared – as Deming proved in his work on quality in post-Second World War Japan – the enterprise becomes self-correcting, self-adapting, self-motivated, able to respond with agility to any changes in needs and context. And thrives as a result.

Science itself has changed, too: the science underlying Taylorist 'scientific management' has long since gone out of date. A present-day 'scientific management' would have to extend beyond the crude concepts of control and cause-and-effect, to include new factors such as recursion, complexity and emergent systems. And in most business contexts, it's not just that those 'human factors' do matter: they *determine* enterprise effectiveness – and the difference between failure and success.

So whilst the machine metaphor leads us naturally towards a focus on efficiency, it leads us *away* from effectiveness – and it's the latter that we really need. Yet however outdated, old metaphors are hard to drop: thinking in terms of the 'living enterprise' may well seem, well, *unnatural*, for a while at least. But it's well worth the effort of persisting with that shift in mindset, because there's a real pay-off in terms of a better understanding of effectiveness, and how to achieve it in practice in the enterprise.

Principles of intervention design

Practice is the real concern here. Metaphors may be interesting, but they're of no use unless we *can* put them to use. Where 'the rubber meets the road' for effectiveness in practice is in the design of diagnostics and interventions that support appropriate change in the enterprise – helping it to become 'efficient on purpose'.

> I'll perhaps risk repeating myself too often here, but it's essential to remember that with the machine metaphor it's all too easy to be 'efficient *without* purpose' – which in real terms is neither efficient nor effective.
>
> It's relatively simple to maximise the efficiency of any one part of 'the machine' on its own, as long as we don't care about the impact anywhere else in the enterprise. It's *not* simple to balance the effectiveness-tradeoffs across the entire enterprise, and keep the whole thing on track towards an intended purpose.
>
> The machine-metaphor beguiles us with that so-desirable delusion that our interventions can provide control over the enterprise – but unfortunately it *is* a delusion. By contrast, the living-enterprise metaphor illustrates the real complexity of what we're dealing with. In designing interventions for a real enterprise, in a real context, with real people, the phrase 'herding cats' comes to mind... but at least it *is* real, which 'the machine' is not.

To the machine-metaphor, the enterprise is simply a scaled-up machine: more and more complicated as it scales in size, but still a machine. So for intervention-design the focus is on 'fail-safe', on certainty, on taking control of causes and effects to create the required, predefined outcomes. Or trying to do so, because it's never really worked...

Instead, the living-enterprise metaphor accepts that complexity is *qualitatively* different. In complex systems, such as in any real-world enterprise, there *is* no certainty; everything is both 'cause' *and* 'effect', so there is no such thing as control. There are definite outcomes, and desirable outcomes at that, but nothing that could be determined for certain in advance. So the emphasis in intervention design is not on 'fail-safe', but *'safe-fail'*.

'Safe-fail' is about deliberate design to 'test the waters', and pull back to a known-safe position if the outcome is not what we want. There is no 'failure' as such, because every intervention is an experiment. And because every intervention is also a diagnostic, this means that, as Dave Snowden of Cognitive Edge puts it, the experiments "allow us to test the evolutionary possibilities of the system", extending our knowledge of what works and what doesn't, within that specific context.

> A simple example here, from quality-systems development.
>
> In conventional control-based models, the emphasis is on 'best-practice' – on replicating exactly what worked well elsewhere. As long as the context *is* the same as elsewhere, that approach does seem to work – mostly, anyway.
>
> But in environments where there are many 'one-offs' and the context inherently uncertain, a better approach is '*worst*-practice'. For example, maintenance-engineers swap stories of what *didn't* work, and the experiments they went through to reach an appropriate solution.
>
> 'Best practice' is always a good idea, wherever we can apply it, but it risks failure as soon as the context moves away from what we and it had expected. And in the real world, ultimately *everything* is a 'market of one': there's always *something* that's a little bit different, in everything we do... Both approaches are valid: the trick – the skill – is in knowing which one to use, where, when and why.

So throughout this book, whenever we talk about intervention-design, it's not about some kind of attempt to 'take control' of this wayward beast we call 'the enterprise'. Rather, it's about working *with* the complexity, often running multiple and sometimes contradictory pilot-projects in parallel, to sense out the responses in the respective business context. Our aim in always to create or extend the enterprise's capabilities – its 'ability to do work', in many different senses – so as to enable an agile response to any changes in conditions, any new opportunities. And by monitoring everything as we go – such as with the SEMPER metric described later – we can amplify whatever works, and quietly dampen what doesn't.

But it *is* a different way of working with the enterprise, a different way of thinking, especially about the role of interventions and actions. It does take a while to get used to it, and to get others used to it, too. There are plenty of practical tools in this book, yet do note that most of them can only work well when combined with this different approach to enterprise effectiveness – please do bear that in mind as you read on!

DIMENSIONS OF EFFECTIVENESS

The dimensions of the enterprise

In the previous chapter we briefly touched on the dimensions of effectiveness; at this point we need to look at them in more depth, to provide a firm foundation for the techniques that follow.

The dimensions of effectiveness mentioned earlier – efficient, reliable, elegant, appropriate, integrated – are linked in turn what are, in effect, another related set of dimensions. In essence, these represent the categories of assets in the enterprise: physical, conceptual, relational and aspirational.

> Yes, I know: yet another bunch of abstract terms. But don't worry about it: the names and details don't matter that much, it's the underlying notion of distinct *dimensions* that matters here.

To illustrate this, imagine the enterprise as a participant in an old-fashioned street-market or bazaar. Within that market, we can see four discrete yet interwoven dimensions:

- there are **transactions** about *physical* products and services – the most visible and evident aspect of the activity in the marketplace;
- there's an exchange of *conceptual* ideas and information – to quote the *Cluetrain Manifesto*, "markets are **conversations**";
- the transactions and conversations help to create and maintain *relational* links between the market's players – and without those interpersonal **relationships**, the market could not operate or exist;
- markets are about identity and **purpose** – the *aspirations* of individuals, and the shared purpose of the market as a whole.

The market is all of these things, all blended together in a kind of bubbling brew of **integration**, distinctive in its own right, which we might call the 'soul' of the market. Hence, in turn, the 'soul' of an enterprise.

Another way to understand these dimensions is in terms of the four classic ways to differentiate an enterprise from its peers and competitors:

- through *products and services* - physical/behavioural
- through *knowledge and innovation* - mental/conceptual
- through *relationships and 'feel'* - emotional/relational
- through *vision and purpose* - spiritual/aspirational

> 'Spiritual' can seem a somewhat risky word in a business context – it tends to bring up the wrong kind of associations with religion and such. Yet though it's obviously relevant to many non-profit organisations such as charities and pressure-groups, it's actually essential for *every* enterprise. The core themes of the aspirational dimension – vision, values, identity, belonging, a sense of meaning and purpose – form the backbone to branding and much of marketing, to internal morale, to commitment and quality, and ultimately to the perceived social 'licence to operate'.
>
> None of this can make any sense whilst we cling to the machine metaphor – after all, a machine has no soul (or no *apparent* soul, at any rate!). But it does make perfect sense once we think in terms of the 'living enterprise' – it's the source of the organisation's drive and creativity. An explicit description of such things becomes a core business asset, so we'll see this often in successful large organisations: Hewlett-Packard's 'HP Way' and Johnson & Johnson's 'Credo' are two well-known examples.

And there's another angle on these same dimensions, through the lens of organisational culture:

- "the way we do things round here" – physical
- "what we know, how we think" – conceptual
- "how we relate with each other, and with others" – relational
- "who we are and what we stand for" – aspirational

It's crucial to understand here that these are *dimensions*, not layers – each is essential to the successful operation of the enterprise, and none of them has any inherent priority over any of the others. Because of this, perhaps the safest way to model the dimensions is as a *tetradian*, the four internal axes of a tetrahedron. Each axis or dimension is held stable by the other three; and by rotating our attention between them, every aspect of the enterprise can come into view. In effect, the tetradian describes the 'innerstructure' or internal skeleton of the enterprise.

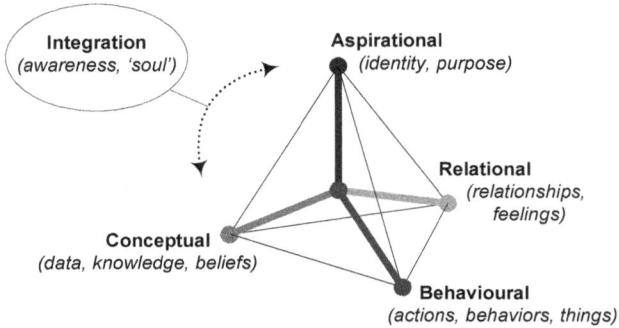

Tetradian model

From this, it's also clear that there are six link-themes that bridge between each pair of dimensions, providing the tension that holds this innerstructure together. We can loosely categorise the forms of these link-themes as follows:

- *vision and values* – linking spiritual/aspirational and emotional/relational
- *skills and leadership* – linking emotional/relational and physical/behavioural
- *active learning* – linking physical/behavioural and mental/conceptual
- *narrative and dialogue* – linking mental/conceptual and emotional/relational
- *sense-making and foresight* – linking mental/conceptual and spiritual/aspirational
- *responsibility and empowerment* – linking spiritual/aspirational and physical/behavioural

If any domain is poorly supported in any part of the organisation, the effectiveness of the overall enterprise is weakened; and if any link-theme is absent altogether, the entire structure will collapse – taking the enterprise down with it. And even if the specialist needs of each domain are adequately represented, the whole still won't work well if there's no generalist integration process to link everything together. Once this is understood, it becomes obvious that appropriate management of innerstructure is essential not just for enterprise effectiveness, but for sustainability and survival.

However, don't expect these domains – the dimensions and link-themes, and the process of integration that links them all together – to map directly to any specific department in an organisation.

Some domains will be more visible in certain departments and business-functions: for example, the HR, sales and marketing departments will emphasise the relational dimension, production and warehousing emphasises the physical, whilst the strategy unit would be more concerned with sense-making and foresight, and perhaps with vision and values. Other domains are more evident at the *boundaries* between departments: who's responsible for leadership development? for innovation and active learning? for the tacit knowledge embedded in narrative and dialogue? The reality is that the innerstructure underpins *everything*. Like infrastructure, only deeper, all the domains necessarily recur in every department and every business-function – and each domain needs appropriate action and support in every context.

Effectiveness acronyms – REAL and LEARN

Given this innerstructure, we can evaluate effectiveness in each domain through four keywords:

- **R**eliable - whether the activity can be relied upon to deliver the required results (maps to the *physical* dimension)
- **E**fficient - whether the activity makes the best use of available resources (maps to the *conceptual* dimension)
- **A**ppropriate - whether the activity supports and sustains the overall purpose of the enterprise (maps to the *aspirational* dimension)
- E**L**egant - whether the activity supports the human factors in the context; also 'elegance' in the scientific sense, in that clarity and the like will support structural simplicity and re-use (maps to the *relational* dimension)

The highlighted letters give us the acronym REAL for the direct dimensions of effectiveness. As we'll see later when we look at the SEMPER metric, we can assess these both in their own right, and cross-mapped to the respective dimension of the innerstructure.

It's also advisable to assess how well each domain, and each activity within each domain, is integrated with the whole – how well it supports the other domains, and is supported by the other domains. This means that we also need to keep track of a kind of 'meta-dimension' that links the other dimensions together:

- **IN**tegrated - whether the activity is linked to and supports the integration of the whole

If we add the highlighted letter to the previous set and give the result a minor tweak, we have the acronym LEARN as a keyword for the effective enterprise – the 'learning organisation'.

It can be relatively easy to assess efficiency and reliability in some domains, using the standard organisational toolkit of techniques built up over the past century. But in practice any overall assessment must inevitably be subjective, at least in part, because so much of the innerstructure is intangible.

Even so, given a consistent methodology and clear guidelines, it's possible to use REAL or LEARN to build a meaningful picture of effectiveness throughout the whole organisation – especially if assessments of different areas, at different times and by different people can be compared, contrasted and consolidated to provide a variety of perspectives on the whole. This is the basis of the SEMPER metric, which we'll explore in detail later – see *SEMPER* (p.49).

Effectiveness in complex systems

The machine-metaphor works well in simple contexts and simple systems. It also works quite well as a way to understand a small sub-component of a large system, as long as the context can be reduced to something reasonably predictable and doesn't have to deal with change. It's convenient, yet it's too simplistic: and as soon as we have to move outside of those artificial constraints, everything starts to fall apart. We find ourselves with intractable problems that keep coming back, sometimes in different forms, no matter how much we try to control them. So to deal with the real complexities of the *real* world, we need something that really does know about complexity.

This is where systems-theory and complexity-science come into the picture – hence the 'living enterprise' metaphor, because it's easiest to understand living organisms when we describe them in terms of complex systems. Unfortunately, most systems-theory is almost impenetrable at first for ordinary people in everyday business: it's often too mathematical, too abstract to make immediate practical sense. Which, since we *need* it in order to understand how to enhance effectiveness, can be something of a problem.

But there is one framework that arose in the business space – out of the knowledge-management domain, in fact – and which *is* easy (or easi*er*) to apply in a business context. Known as Cynefin –

apparently a Welsh word loosely translated as 'place' – it was originally developed by Dave Snowden and others at IBM, and was later spun-off to a separate company, Cognitive Edge. It provides us with a visual summary of the different approaches we need to deal with different contexts in real-world complexity:

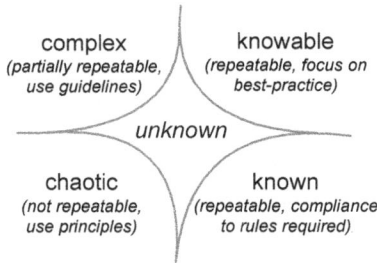

```
         complex          |          knowable
   (partially repeatable, /|\  (repeatable, focus on
      use guidelines)    /   \     best-practice)
  _____<  unknown  >_____
                         \         /
         chaotic          \       /      known
   (not repeatable,        \|/  (repeatable, compliance
      use principles)       |     to rules required)
```

Cynefin model of context complexity

When we first start to look at a context, everything is in that central region of the 'unknown'. We then have four distinct modes or domains for sense-making: recognise it as known; find some way to make it knowable in an ordered way; accept its inherent complexity; or accept it as an unique 'market of one'.

In the *known domain* everything is assumed to comply with simple, explicit, clearly-identifiable rules – the kind of ordered world that legislation and regulation would expect. There's no need to stop and think: all we have to do here is sense the context, categorise, and respond in accordance with the respective rule.

> This is usually the preferred approach in a production environment, if only because there's often no *time* to stop and think. The catch is that it'll fall apart if it meets up with anything that can't fit the rules.
>
> On one of our assignments we worked with a large security organisation which – true to type – was almost obsessive about strict compliance with rules. "But what happens if there's an event that doesn't fit the rules?", we asked.
>
> "Easy – we make up another rule!"
>
> "Yes, but *when* do you make up the new rule?"
>
> "After the event, I suppose."
>
> "So how do you handle the event itself, since you don't have a rule for it at the time?"
>
> An *interesting* silence…

In the *knowable domain*, an ordered world of cause-and-effect is still assumed, but it's accepted that simple rules aren't enough – it's *complicated*. This is the preferred domain of the specialist, the analyst, the management consultant – the white-collar workers, the outsider 'brain' in the Taylorist machine-metaphor. The key tactic here is 'sense, analyse, respond', so there needs to be time to think – though we have to be careful to avoid 'analysis paralysis'.

At some point we hit 'complication overload', and move into the *complex domain*. Here we accept that no matter how much we'd like the world to conform to our predefined rules and analyses, reality is that much of the time it doesn't. So the tactic here is 'probe, sense, respond', guided by skill, experience, heuristics, the occasional 'rule of thumb'. Here we'd run multiple experiments in parallel, in a 'safe-fail' context, and pick out the most successful – most 'elegant' – solutions from their results. Although we look for a kind of truth here – and will often switch back and forth between this and the 'knowable' domain, to analyse our results – the emphasis is not on '*the* truth' but '*a* truth', a self-adapting pattern that we can re-use with agility in many different ways.

> A good example here is weather forecasting. For a long while it was hoped that we would be able to identify '*the* rules', *the* science – however complicated – by which the weather *really* worked. Unfortunately, the realities of chaos-mathematics and the 'butterfly effect' put an end to that delightful deterministic dream … oh well…
>
> But we still have accurate weather forecasts – and they're improving every year. What's happened is that they still use the same massively complicated equations: but instead of looking for '*the* one true forecast', forecasters run multiple, parallel computations, with small differences in their setup parameters, each leading to '*a* possibly-true forecast'. When several simulations converge on the same overall pattern, that's the most probable weather outcome. It's complex – but it works, where analysis alone did not.

At the point of contact there's always *something* that's somewhat different, that doesn't fit any rule at all: ultimately everything is in some way a unique 'market of one'. This is the *chaotic domain*, and the key tactic here is one of 'act, sense, respond'. In the knowable domain we have time for analysis, and in the complex domain we still have time to try out our experiments, but here, as in the known domain, we no longer have that luxury: we have to act now, and fast! But where the known domain assumes everything is the same, and must be made to fit the rules, here we know that the rules won't work, or at least won't make sense: often here our principles and aspirations become the only reliable guide.

As a guideline – though it's not part of the Cynefin model as such – the domains do map approximately to the dimensions of effectiveness as follows:

- known-domain (rules): physical dimension; reliable
- knowable-domain (analyses): conceptual dimension; efficient
- complex-domain (heuristics): relational dimension; elegant
- chaotic-domain (principles): aspirational dimension; appropriate

In the real world of everyday business, effectiveness will depend greatly on choosing the appropriate Cynefin domain and the respective tactics to guide decision-making. For example, trying to apply rigid rules and regulations to a complex- or chaotic-domain context is never going to work well. Instead, we need to identify which parts of the context *can* be governed by rules, and which parts require heuristic- or principle-driven flexibility.

Cynefin domains also indicate the required level of skill in each context. For a rule-bound context – in other words, the known-domain – routine training should usually suffice; but analytical skill would be needed in the knowable-domain, whilst extensive experience is essential to work well in the complex-domain, and an even higher level of skill in the chaotic-domain.

Another useful business-oriented source on systems thinking is the books by Peter Sengé and his colleagues on the concept and practice of the 'learning organisation' – *The Fifth Discipline*, *The Fifth Discipline Fieldbook* and *The Dance of Change*. Although the first book is perhaps a bit too heavy on theory for many people's taste, the others are more like practical 'cookbooks', filled with concrete practical examples of the 'learning organisation' – a key attribute of enterprise effectiveness.

Reviewing relevance

The tetradian provides a view of the innerstructure of a given context, and the REAL and LEARN keywords provide a means to assess it. To enhance effectiveness, though, it's also necessary to understand the relevance of each part in the overall context, and how issues in one context can be leveraged, balanced and traded off with other contexts in order to optimise the workings of the whole.

This is where we put systems-theory into practice. The main techniques to do this are embodied in a set of principles adapted from complexity-science, denoted by the acronym **R⁵**:

- _Rotation_ – look at the context from diverse perspectives
- _Recursion_ – look for ways in which similar issues recur at different scales
- _Reciprocation_ – look for balance or imbalance in transactions
- _Resonance_ – look for the 'snowball effect' through which results tend to increase (positive-feedback) or decrease (damping) automatically over time
- _Reflexion_ – look for ways in which the whole can be seen even in the smallest part

The R⁵ principles are used both in assessment and in intervention design.

Rotation is fairly straightforward: the aim is to gain a better under-standing of the context than would be available from a single perspective. However, this often involves dealing with contra-diction and conflict, as the views may well be different but are equally 'true' from their own perspective. The tetradian itself is an example of a rotation, providing different views of the organis-ation's innerstructure from the perspective of each domain. Other examples include looking at the organisation from the viewpoint of each department, or from different operational levels, or from the perspectives of other stakeholders such as suppliers, custom-ers, investors, government and the wider community.

Recursion is helpful because it can highlight options to simplify processes and remove costly and ineffective 'special cases'. It can also simplify training: recursion creates systems and structures that are much the same at many different levels and in different contexts, making it much easier to move people around as needed with only minimal context-specific training. The simplest business example of recursion is the reporting-hierarchy of the infamous 'org-chart': each person reports upward and has their own reports downward in the hierarchy-tree. A more sophisticated example is Stafford Beer's Viable Systems Model, which was applied to the public service of an entire country – Allende's Chile – and proved to be remarkably adaptable and resilient even under wartime con-ditions. Recursion is important in assessment, too, to review how issues affect one another at different scales, from the individual level, through work-group and business-unit, to the whole enter-

16

prise, the wider community and other interactions right up to the global scale.

Reciprocation addresses two subtly different types of balance. At the tangible level, the standard models of classical physics apply: everything has to balance out. The catch, as general systems theory demonstrates, is that the balance - or re-balancing of any asymmetry - may be complex and difficult to decipher, often involving delays that span days or decades, or transformations from one type of energy to another. For most intangible assets, though, the balance is not a simple 'win/lose', but something closer to a choice between 'win/win' or 'lose/lose': either every-one wins, or everyone loses. Making sense of this type of symmetry depends on a radically different concept of power and responsibility, derived from the physics definition that 'power is the ability to do work', rather than the common social definitions which seem more to imply that power is the ability to *avoid* work. (For more detail on the power-model used in SEMPER, refer to the glossary entries for 'power' and 'responsibility', and the related terms such as 'power-with' and 'power-against' – see *Appendix A: Glossary*, p.127.) To assess this form of reciprocation, the focus is less on the surface appearances and appurtenances of 'power', or on who is purported to have it or not have it, but more on the type of work to be done, and the availability of the various types of energies and resources – physical, conceptual, relational, aspir-ational – which the work requires.

Resonance is the exception to that reciprocal balance – the feedback loops which can be found in all complex real-world systems. In systems-theory this can occur through 'positive feedback' or feed-forward – both of which increase the 'snowball effect' towards self-propagation – or as 'negative feedback', or damping, which reduces the effect. See Peter Sengé's *The Fifth Discipline* for more on this, for example.

Reflexion is more complex – literally so, as it's one of the most important yet counter-intuitive concepts from complexity science. This is the holographic sense that every part, every place, every action in the enterprise somehow also contains within itself every other part of the enterprise. Identifying reflexion takes experience and an eye for detail, but it can save enormous amounts of time and effort in assessment and intervention design: as the eminent consultant Gerry Weinberg put it, "I always get the answer in the first five minutes – though it may take me hours or days or weeks to recognise what it was that I saw in those first five minutes!" One example is the way that the real values – not just the espoused values – of an enterprise and its culture are revealed in every conversation, every transaction, every workplace, every department, even though the surface similarities in each case may be small.

Together, these elements – dimensions, domains, complexity and relevance – comprise an overall framework to enhance enterprise effectiveness. From here we can start to put it into practice. First, though, we need to simplify it one more step. We do so by re-structuring our key four elements to five – as described in the next chapter.

FIVE ELEMENTS

Time, workflow and process

The tetradian in its standard tetrahedral form is a powerful tool for analysts and consultants, as we'll see later, for example, with the full SEMPER diagnostic. We can rotate the tetradian in any direction, to give us different views on the whole enterprise. Yet at the concrete level of day-to-day business, it can at first seem too abstract for immediate use. To apply it at 'the coalface', we'll often need to link it more closely to time, workflow and business process.

One way to do this arises from the fact that the conceptual dimension has two different emphases: looking forward to the near future – plans and preparations – and looking back at the past, at what has been done. This allows us to flatten out the tetradian into a single business-oriented cycle of five elements or **5Ps**: Purpose, People, Preparation, Process, Performance.

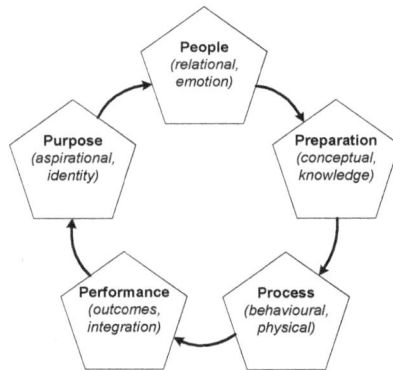

5Ps: the project cycle

This is essentially the same as Bruce Tuckman's 'Group Dynamics' sequence: Forming, Storming, Norming, Performing, Adjourning. Proven in practice for more than fifty years, this well-known description of the project life-cycle can be found in any entry-level management text-book. The sequence explains not only the 'natural' steps of the life-cycle, but what happens in we try to miss

19

out any of the steps – such as the chaos that ensues if we try to jump straight from idea to practice without dealing with the people-issues ('Storming') or a proper plan ('Norming').

The difference here is that the 5Ps have the added dimensions of effectiveness and relevance – in effect, merging Group Dynamics with systems-theory. Where Group Dynamics describes a life-sequence for a single project, the 5Ps form a true *cycle* where the end of each project is also the start of another. And it's recursive, reflexive, reciprocal and the rest: project-cycles contain and are contained within other project-cycles, all the way up to the enterprise as a whole.

> Interestingly, this also maps exactly to another, much older framework: the classic Chinese 'Five Elements' of Wood, Fire, Earth, Metal, Water. The elements have complex relationships that can be supportive or destructive: for example, Wood feeds Fire, breaks up Earth, fractures Metal, dams Water. Of all the possible combinations of relationships, the sequence Wood → Fire → Earth → Metal → Water is the only one in which each element naturally supports the next – and it's an exact metaphor of the sequence in Group Dynamics.
>
> As consultants, that mapping has provided us with many valuable insights into what would otherwise have been intractable business issues. For an example, see the section later about *Five Elements in business analysis* (p.32).

We can summarise the 5Ps from a business perspective as follows:

Purpose ('Forming'; 'Wood')

- *Role perspective*: "why?" – vision, values, purpose, identity; core principles for decision-making
- *Time focus*: mid- to far-future
- *Business-context examples*: policy & strategy, R&D, product development

People ('Storming'; Fire')

- *Role perspective*: "who?" – roles, skills, experience, quality of internal relationships and trust
- *Time focus*: mixed (past ↔ future)
- *Business-context examples*: HR, marketing

Preparation ('Norming'; 'Earth')

- *Role perspective*: "which to do? what to do? when to do? where to do? how to do?" – knowledge, planning, mindsets, beliefs
- *Time focus*: near future

- *Business-context examples*: planning, scheduling and logistics, purchasing, supplies

Process ('Performing'; 'Metal')

- *Role perspective*: "is!" (no time for questions!) – resources, actions, environments
- *Time focus*: immediate – "now!"
- *Business-context examples*: production, sales

Performance ('Adjourning'; 'Water')

- *Role perspective*: "which was done? what was done? when was it done? where was it done? how was it done?" - bringing it all together, completions, lessons-learned, 'calling to account'
- *Time focus*: past
- *Business-context examples*: accounts, quality assurance, despatch

Although the mapping is not as exact as with Group Dynamics or the Chinese five elements, there's another useful cross-reference to the Total Quality Management (TQM) cycle Plan → Do → Check → Act. TQM's 'Plan' phase is much the same as 5Ps 'Preparation', and 'Do' is obviously similar to 'Process'. TQM's 'Check' straddles across both 'Performance' and the transition to the new cycle at 'Purpose', whilst the mapping for TQM's 'Act' is rather more blurred, from 'Purpose' to aspects of 'People', and even to 'Preparation' again at the strategic rather than tactical level. Because 5Ps is linked so strongly to systems-theory, this gives us a means to link existing quality-management efforts to a more recursive and reflexive view of the enterprise as a whole – a valuable tool in enterprise architecture.

But where the 5Ps model really scores is that it provides a means to understand and resolve internal conflict within the enterprise. It does so by showing how the perspective on *time* will change during the project life-cycle which impacts not only on workflow and process, but on what should otherwise be supportive relationships between the different departments that are responsible for the different phases of the overall workflow. To understand those conflicts – and what to do to resolve them – we need to develop an *experiential* understanding of those five perspectives.

Five perspectives – an exercise on conflict

One of the most visible factors impacting on enterprise effective-ness is interpersonal conflicts – especially all those arguments, or feuds even, that rage between the different departments of the enterprise. Reducing those conflicts would make everyone's life a lot easier, and go a long way towards getting a lot more done...

The key insight here is that although some conflict does arise from personality-clashes, much if not most arises from differences in role-perspectives and role-timeframes – it's not that others are being 'awkward' or whatever, but that *the differences arise from the natural flow of work through the project lifecycle*. The conflicts are inevitable, inherent in the work itself, so there's no way we can prevent them as such; but what we *can* do is take the heat of them.

So here's an exercise using the 5Ps – purpose, people, preparation, pocess and performance – as a framework to assess and resolve role-based conflict. The overall aim is to show – and *experience* – how to improve overall effectiveness of the enterprise by accept-ing and working with the natural conflicts and natural flows in work. For the workshop itself, you'll need the usual whiteboard and a meeting-space that permits clustering of participants into five groups.

Part 1: Effectiveness and conflict

Our objectives in this part are to identify criteria for personal, group and collective success, and to identify differences between individual and group definitions of success.

The key concepts we introduce here are the notion of effectiveness as 'efficient and on purpose'; and the layering of definitions of 'success' – personal, group (department), collective (organisation) and so on.

Step 1: Introduce self and participants

This should be the usual quick thirty-seconds-per-person intro-duction of participants – who they are, their backgrounds, roles, expectations and the like.

Step 2: Situation, complication, question, answer

Introduce the topics for the workshop, using the classic frame of 'situation, complication, question, answer'. Allow perhaps fifteen minutes overall for this.

The situation: every organisation wants to be effective – to achieve and sustain high performance – in whatever way performance may be measured.

- How would you know when you're effective, when you've succeeded? How do you define success? (layers of success: organisational, departmental, personal)

> Elicit opinions, anecdotes and experiences on this; cluster some of these on the whiteboard.
>
> Hint towards links between *definition* of success (Purpose) and *measurement* of success (Performance).

The complication: to a greater or lesser extent, the effectiveness of the enterprise is constrained and limited by fragmentation and by interpersonal and inter-departmental conflicts.

- What are some of these constraints and conflicts?

> As before, elicit opinions, anecdotes and experiences on this, clustering as appropriate on the whiteboard

The question: Is this happening just because people are awkward? Are they deliberately sabotaging success? Or what?

> Once more, elicit opinions, anecdotes and experiences on this, creating clusters on the whiteboard.
>
> Summarise, then lead to:

An answer: No, it's mostly because they each look at the world from different perspectives and with different time-frames – and don't realise that the view isn't the same for everyone else. Most of the conflicts are *natural*, arising from the nature of the work itself.

Part 2: The structure of conflict

The objective for this part is to distinguish between direct interpersonal conflict, and contextual conflict that arises from roles and timeframes.

This is where we introduce the key concepts for the exercise itself: that although some conflict arises from personality-clashes (which we're not dealing with here), most conflict in organisations arises from role-perspectives and role-timeframes; and that we can use the 5Ps framework to assess and resolve this role-based conflict.

Step 1: The structure of organisations

Allow about ten minutes overall for this step. A typical introductory script would be as follows:

We'd like to show you a simple framework and set of techniques to address the conflicts that arise from different perspectives. These will:

- give you a direct *experience* of integration, of working within a whole
- give you a better grasp of where your and others' work fits within the whole
- help to reduce conflicts
- improve overall effectiveness.

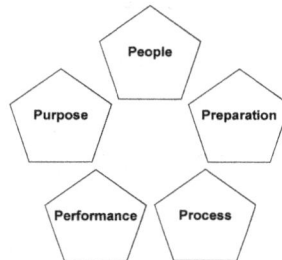

People

Purpose   Preparation

Performance   Process

Business labels for Five Elements

Describe the structure and functions of your enterprise in terms of these five categories:

- *Purpose*: beginnings, ideas, future
- *People*: energy, expression, the 'interpersonal stuff'
- *Preparation*: settling down, getting ready, getting everything in its place
- *Process*: doing it, often with lots of noise!
- *Performance*: completions, wrapping up, tidying up all the loose ends

> Elicit descriptions of these labels as departments or business-units within the organisation, so that they can claim the 5Ps labels as something of their own. Write these descriptions against the label-names on the whiteboard.

Create business-oriented 5P labels for each table or table-cluster.

> Place the label on the respective table or cluster as each label is described.

Step 2: Same and different at every level

In this brief five-minute step we would introduce the scaling issue of recursion: each of these domains – as per the labels from the previous step – also includes all of the other 5Ps domains within itself. For example, a production environment would – or should – also include within itself its own purpose, people, preparation and performance sub-domains, and so on, almost ad infinitum.

Step 3: One view of the world

Here we start to build not just the idea but the *feeling* of contextual view. To do this, we get each group to describe their view of themselves and others, in terms of the work-context.

> We don't want to pre-empt the shift of feeling that happens in the next step, so warn people that if they're sitting at a table or cluster that's labelled with their usual work-role, this would be a good time to move somewhere else!

Going round the clusters, ask participants to describe:

- the priorities, concerns and constraints from within 'their' cluster
- their view of each of the other clusters – being as happily rude as they like!

> Laughter is important here. It should be safe to use – in fact encourage – pejorative terms, because no-one's sitting in their 'usual' role, but do be careful to dissuade any direct *personal* attacks and to use laughter to diffuse any tension. Emphasise the stereotype-labels for each grouping of 'others' – 'the people-people', 'the bean-counters' and so on – to reduce the risk of attacks on individuals.
>
> Elicit comments about relative time-frames, but don't make this explicit as yet.
>
> Put selected statements up on the whiteboard, showing the vectors to each cluster.

At the end, the summary from the whiteboard should show that:

- everyone has a clear view of their own work – of what the enterprise needs, from the perspective of that 5Ps label
- from each perspective, everyone is certain that they are right
- everyone else is wrong!

Step 4: All move round one

Having been happily rude to everyone else, it's now time to explore how it feels to be on the receiving-end.

> Before we do this, we need everyone to move around to a different space, either literally or metaphorically. Either move the participants round one to the next table, or allow them to move at random, but in any case to a different cluster; or else move the labels round one. (The

> latter usually doesn't work so well – if only because getting people to move around also usefully lifts the group-energy – but practical constraints such as seating in a lecture theatre may make it necessary in some environments.)

Read back the *incoming* views of each cluster – those 'happily rude' descriptions from the previous step. Ask how it *feels* to be described by others in that way.

> We're looking for phrases like "they're being unfair", or "they don't understand what we do". Emphasise these as they come up, particularly where the same feeling is expressed by different groups.

Summarise as follows:

- the sense of feeling misunderstood and the like by others is *universal*.
- the 'unfairness' comes not from those other people as such, but from the *natural* view from that the role – especially when the perspective is thought of as 'the only right view'

This shows us that many of the conflicts we deal with at work are the *natural* result of different perspectives:

- a 'de Bono-ism': "everyone is always right [from their own perspective] but no-one's ever right" [because no one perspective can see the whole]

When we remember to look at 'the world' from other perspectives, we immediately reduce the tension in the conflicts – and immediately *increase* the overall effectiveness.

Part 3: Conflicting timeframes

The objectives in this part are to become aware of differences in timeframes, and to distinguish between the *local* validity of each timeframes versus the dangers of the *universal* application of a single timeframe.

The key concepts we introduce here are that each role-perspective also has its own specific timeframe, and that conflicts can arise from unrecognised differences in timeframes.

Step 1: Timeframes

What we'll explore here is that the clashes arise not just from different perspectives, but also different *timeframes*.

Allow ten minutes or so to go round each cluster, eliciting descriptions and comments.

> Place summaries from each cluster on the respective section of the whiteboard. The aim should be to end up with something like the following list:
>
> *Purpose*: mid- to far-future
>
> *People*: random, 'all over the place'
>
> *Preparation*: near future
>
> *Process*: "*now!*"
>
> *Performance*: past

Referencing these descriptions, go round each cluster again, asking what would happen if they try to do the respective activity from the wrong timeframe.

> Essentially what we're after is a sense that if we do this, there'd be total chaos and ineffectiveness.

Indicate that this is what happens when one perspective dominates – when there's only 'one right view' in the enterprise.

Step 2: Only one view

Go round each cluster, eliciting comments from the whole group about what would happen (or *does* happen) if one perspective were to dominate the enterprise. Allow ten minutes or so to do this. Take care to ensure that comments are aimed to the *role*, and to deflect comments away from the participants currently sitting 'in' that role. For example, stand at each place, and encourage comments to be aimed at self rather than at the cluster.

> What we're after are examples such as the following (in element order):
>
> *Purpose*: "dreamers and 'idea-hamsters' run the place": nothing gets started, let alone finished.
>
> *People*: "people-issues run the place": a lot of activity but nothing much actually happens; instead, there are endless discussions about who might do what, or who might get what – or, worse, the place is dominated by interpersonal politics and jockeying for position.
>
> *Preparation*: "planners run the place": the place gets stuck in 'analysis paralysis'.
>
> *Process*: "production managers run the place": everything is *now!*, urgent, no forward or (often) even backward view.
>
> *Performance*: "accountants run the place": everything is focussed on performance indicators and the backward view.

Notice also that the dominant element tends to be different for different types of enterprise:

- *Purpose*: academics and think-tanks

- *People, Preparation*: government organisations and non-profits
- *Process, Performance*: commercial organisations

Separate into small groups (not necessarily on cluster boundaries) to identify which elements dominate in their own enterprise, how this affects their own work and their *personal* commitment to the work, and how they do or can resolve the clashes. Allow perhaps fifteen minutes for this discussion

> Either during or at the end of the discussion-period, invite participants to provide summaries, comments and suggestions to put up on the whiteboard. Cluster the comments around each of the five elements on the board such that there is a visible gap remaining in the centre.
>
> The aim here is that the participants should themselves notice the gap – for example, at one of our workshops, a senior executive suddenly blurted out, "Hang on, who's in the centre?" If this doesn't happen, allude to it during the wrap-up for this step.

Summarise by showing that a single view tends to dominate when the work of the enterprise itself tends to emphasise that view – giving the illusion that that one view is 'the right one', or at least should always have the final say. This also occurs where there is poor communication between perspectives, as in the classic 'silos' scenario.

But if – as the participants themselves have just demonstrated – real problems arise if one view is allowed to dominate, this leads naturally to an important question:

Step 3: Who's minding the store?

Who's holding the centre? Who is responsible for ensuring that the baton is passed cleanly between each of the perspectives, in a mutually-supportive workflow? Who's responsible for ensuring that one perspective *doesn't* ride roughshod over all the others? Who's responsible for resolving the perspective-conflicts that we've explored in the workshop?

The short answer, in far too many organisations, is *no-one* – which is precisely why there's a problem… There's an essential role here for a generalist, a communicator, someone who has enough grasp of *all* of the perspectives so as to be able to translate between them. Or several roles, rather, since the same need will recur all the way from the top – where ideally, if rarely, the CEO is exactly this kind of generalist – right down to the 'coal-face'.

The catch is that, especially at the more delivery-oriented levels, personal performance is usually measured in specialist terms – in terms of one perspective. So the more these generalists do their 'communicator' role, the less they appear to do, from the point of view of that single perspective – "they do nothing but talk all day! distracting us from *real* work! we don't have time for this stuff!" – and hence may well be penalised for *improving* the effectiveness of the overall enterprise. To do *their* 'real work', generalists will often need protection and support all the way from the top – and their performance measured in terms of the whole, rather than any one part.

Split the participants into small discussion groups to explore these issues:

- who are the generalists and 'translators' in the enterprise?
- what official labels – if any – are assigned to their 'communicator' or 'translator' roles? to whom do they report, and how and why?
- what support – if any – do they have in those roles? is the support covert, or officially sanctioned – a typical tacit "do what you can and we'll cover up for you", or a formally authorised role with its own performance-metrics? what can be done to move the support from the former to the latter?
- what else could be done in the enterprise to support this need to 'hold the centre'?

As before, allow perhaps fifteen minutes for this discussion.

> Add to the whiteboard the summaries, comments and suggestions from the groups, showing also how some roles and activities act as 'ambassadors' between specific perspectives and the centre, or between perspectives.

To wrap up, show that what's been built up on the whiteboard is a summary of the whole 'living enterprise', with a clear sense of its future, acting in the now, and aware of its past – and accepting people *as* people, too. If there are imbalances visible there – which is usually the case – it now should be clear what needs to be done to resolve them.

Part 4: Working with conflict

This section isn't part of the workshop as such, but is a practical way to show how to work *with* this natural conflict rather than trying to suppress it.

The objectives here are to show other practical applications for the Five Elements (5Ps) framework, and to develop the ability to switch between perspectives and timeframes as appropriate.

The key concepts we emphasise here are that there is a natural flow between the 5Ps, and that the 'communicators' in the enterprise need to be able to work with and translate between each of the perspectives and timeframes.

Steps: Working with the conflict

We've seen that many of the conflicts in organisations arise as a *natural* consequence of the perspectives and timeframes. We've also seen the problems that arise if any one perspective tends to dominate, or if the roles in the transitions between elements are missed.

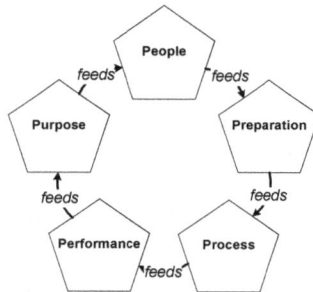

Direct supportive flow around the elements

So what follows is a way to use the Five Elements to keep track of the whole. It's especially useful as a meeting-management framework – somewhat like de Bono's 'Six Hats' – but it also works well as a quick summary and checklist in any context.

Go through each of the elements *in sequence*. In a meeting, the *whole group* works with one element at a time (much like 'Six Hats'). Within your group, select a current business-issue, and assess it in terms of these elements:

- *Purpose*: What's the purpose here? What are we aiming to do? What is the perspective in the timeframe of mid- to far-future? (Use the question of identity – Who is 'We' here? – to move towards People.)
- *People*: Who do we have? What are their skills and experience, interests, concerns, availability? What alliances do we need? What are the interpersonal issues? What changes in perspective occur as the timeframe swings around here, from

far-past to far-future and back again? (Return to skills and availability, and integrate with the Purpose-issues, to move towards Preparation.)

- *Preparation*: What's the plan? What resources, skills, experience, alliances do we have available? What's the perspective from the time-frame of the near-future? (Return to the plan, and integrate with the Purpose-issues and People-issues, to move towards Process.)
- *Process*: What are we doing – right *now*? How does what we do in each moment affect the other timeframes of future and past? How do we minimise distractions from other timeframes, other perspectives? (Focus on how to keep track of what's happening, of what's been done and not done, as work progresses, to integrate with the previous issues of Purpose, People and Preparation, and move towards Performance.)
- *Performance*: What have we done? How do we measure success, in terms of each of the elements? What lessons can we learn from what's been done? (Use the focus on 'lessons learned' to integrate back with Purpose, People, Preparation and Process, and move on to a new cycle at Purpose.)

Some other questions to consider:

- What are the elements (or 5Ps) here? What capabilities and needs do we have in each domain? Who is responsible for each domain?
- What are the flows, in time and space, between each domain?
- How do we manage the inherent differences of perspective between the domains?
- What support do we provide for leading transitions between elements?
- What support do we provide for 'holding the centre'? Who is responsible for 'holding the centre'?

> Ask for comments, suggestions and insights. Place these up on the whiteboard in five-element format.

On completion, work with the group to derive decisions as appropriate from the summaries on the whiteboard.

Wrap up the meeting with a 'lessons learned' section – in other words the Performance phase, or Group Dynamics' 'Adjourning' – to summarise not only the outcome of the meeting, but also any insights from the process itself.

(See the *Real Enterprise Architecture* book for examples of how to use the same principles on a much larger scale, at the level of the whole enterprise.)

Five Elements in business analysis

Another use for Five Elements is in workflow analysis. Every path through a business-process is also a kind of mini-project in its own right, with its own 5Ps sequence of Purpose, People, Preparation, Process and Performance. If we move the view upward, it then becomes possible to see the entire enterprise as a web of inter-connected services – the 'service-oriented enterprise'. Different workgroups provide each other with the respective 5Ps services.

What happens, though, when the enterprise focus is on one of the 5Ps, and it tries to merge with a group that has a different focus? That's what occurred with a client of ours – leading to a simmering conflict that at first seemed bizarre and inexplicable. But when we used a Five Elements approach to describe the situation, it not only became immediately obvious what was going on, but also what to do to make the merger work.

The enterprise was a large government research facility with an enviable international reputation in its field. The government of the day was doing one of its periodic purges, shedding full-time employees and pushing the work out to commercial service-providers. Although the facility itself wasn't much affected by this, there was a risk of losing essential experience from the field – so a few key groups of field-engineers were 'protected' from privatisation by moving them under the aegis of the laboratory.

It had seemed a good idea at the time, such an obvious solution to the problem: "they're all technical types, they'll get on like a house on fire!", one of the senior executives had said to us. But the arguments started within days, and grew more and more acrimonious as the weeks went by...

Yes, true, they were all 'technical types': but no-one had thought about the subtle differences – especially time-perspectives. "We get a job out in three days", snapped one of the engineers; "that lot over there can barely get a report out in three *years!*" From their side, the scientists complained that the engineers were inflexible, sticking rigidly to the rule-book even when it didn't make sense, and tending to act first and think later - "if at all", muttered one disgruntled researcher. It was not a happy time...

Once we applied a Five Elements approach, though, it was clear straight away what was happening. By their nature, scientists are all about Purpose, the future, the uncertainty of new ideas and new beginnings. And the engineers, by *their* nature, are all about certainty, hard fact, concrete action, the immediacy of *'Now!'*. In the classic Chinese terms, one is Wood, the other is Metal: not a good combination, to say the least.

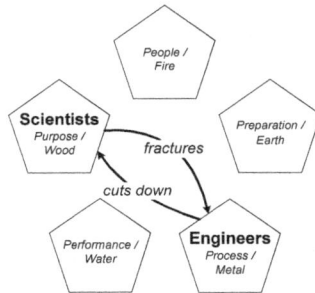

Research-establishment merger: elements out of balance

Even worse, there's an inherent asymmetry in the relationship: Wood eventually fractures Metal, but Metal quickly chops down Wood. By the very nature of their work and time-perspective, the engineers would have a disproportionate impact on the entire establishment. Yet no-one would acknowledge that there was a problem: which meant that – again in Chinese terms – the Fire of interpersonal conflicts went further and further out of control.

The solution was not to try to stop the conflict as such, but to 'fill in the gaps' – in other words, emphasise the rest of the Five Elements, in their 'supportive flow' sequence:

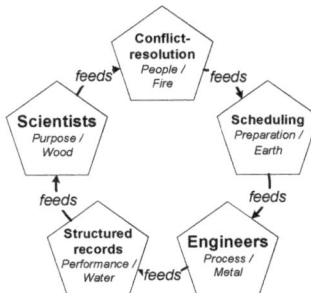

Research-establishment merger: elements in balance

For the Fire or 'People' element, we set up a formal procedure (the engineers *liked* formal procedures!) for conflict-resolution between the two groups. This was nothing special: a couple of written procedures to outline roles and responsibilities; a regular meeting to review the overall work-relationship between the two groups; and an escalation process to handle day-to-day issues. The key point here was to acknowledge that the conflicts were a natural and necessary consequence of the work: the scientists *needed* flexibility, the engineers *needed* structure, so there would always be conflicts there. So no-one was 'wrong' for being in conflict with others in that sense, it was just something to be respected and addressed as a routine aspect of the work. Simple, yet it worked really well: it took the heat out of the overall conflict in a matter of days.

Next, for Earth, or the 'Preparation' element, we adapted the engineers' scheduling system to a shared tool for communication between the two groups. Again, we could implement this at very low cost: we converted their existing spreadsheet to a database, and added an off-the-shelf intranet front-end with a wiki-type hook-up that allowed both groups to add and exchange comments about project-schedules. This also made it possible for researchers to slot small experiments into the engineers' workload in a predictable way, without disrupting their routine work – removing what had previously been a major source of contention.

The final missing element was Water, or 'Performance' – in this case, the 'lessons-learned' records via which the engineers' work could support that of the researchers. This was more difficult, because all work-results had to be recorded and stored in a structured way which emphasised not just the final report – all that was required by the engineers' usual end-clients – but also inputs and outputs of all the intermediate process-steps – which was what the researchers needed, to feed into their own analyses. But here we were able to leverage off some previous work for a workflow / database system for another major project elsewhere in the laboratory, which defined all the data-structures and workflow meta-structures that we needed. The structured framework also made it easier to develop process-documentation for formal accreditation of the engineers' quality-system.

With this support for the missing elements in place, relationships between the two groups shifted from mutual conflict to mutual support – a happy outcome all round, and one that definitely enhanced the overall effectiveness of the enterprise.

SCORE FOR STRATEGY

SCORE for strategic assessment

Strategy is where the enterprise identifies its first moves towards a desired future. This isn't solely an issue for a separate 'strategy team' for senior executives: as we've seen, the 'brain of the firm' is distributed throughout the enterprise. So to enhance effectiveness, the tetradian's Aspirational dimension (or the Five Elements' 'Purpose' domain) needs appropriate support in *every* activity, at *every* level. Strategy occurs *everywhere*.

The classic checklist for quick strategic assessments is SWOT: Strengths, Weaknesses, Opportunities, Threats. (If you're not familiar with this, you can look it up in almost any management textbook.) It's a useful tool, but it does have some real limitations, especially around the impact of strategy on overall effectiveness. Rethinking SWOT as SCORE gives us a versatile alternative with a stronger emphasis on effectiveness, and gives us a chance to test out in practice some of the principles we've seen so far.

So it's useful to explore in brief the constraints of SWOT, and how SCORE resolves those limitations. Here we'll look at how to use SCORE in practice, and end with a real-world SCORE example, about data-architecture strategy in the utilities industry.

Like SWOT, SCORE is an acronym for a strategy checklist:

- Strengths
- Challenges
- Options
- Responses
- Effectiveness

We focus in turn on our Strengths; our Challenges; our Options and opportunities; the probable Responses and returns of the strategy; and the impact on overall Effectiveness.

Another difference is that we're also looking for anything we can measure, either qualitative or quantitative – hence "What's the SCORE?". And we do the same assessment before *and* after we apply the strategy – which tells us whether or not the strategy actually worked.

Critique of SWOT

Why rethink SWOT? After all, it's been around for decades, and it's easy to understand and use. It has the same kind of two-axis matrix beloved by consultants everywhere – in this case, assets versus concerns, and 'internal' versus 'external' relative to the enterprise. And its methodology is about as simple as it gets: tick the boxes, and you're just about done. "Strengths? Weaknesses? Opportunities? Threats? Everything look okay? Right, let's do it!"

	asset	concern
internal	strength	weakness
external	opportunity	threat

SWOT – a classic two-axis matrix

SWOT is great for a quick check. But its subtle yet serious limitations do create real problems in developing strategy, and in devolving that strategy into tactics.

One is that some of its language can be pejorative and misleading, and introduces a spurious sense of danger – literally, of weakness, or of threat. 'Weakness' also implies inadequacy, 'not good enough' and so on – which can be awkward when we're assessing people-issues.

It also creates an arbitrary boundary between 'inside' and 'outside'. This isn't helpful when the boundary between 'us and them' is blurred – as it must be, for example, in value-webs or end-to-end networks where our customers may also be our suppliers, or in consortia where our nominal competitors are also our partners.

And SWOT doesn't really have the breadth of scope to cope with whole-of-system context, or continuity over time. Issues tend to be viewed in isolation, as strategy for *this* single issue, ignoring its broader background. The process tends to be used 'once-off', then forgotten: in some cases it may be repeated, but there's no explicit requirement to create links between repetitions.

So to make SWOT more useful in today's more complex world, we need to make the language more real – not 'weaknesses' or 'threats'. We need to adapt it for use in broader, more complex contexts, in which boundaries between 'inside' and 'outside' may be blurred by multi-organisation partnerships and value-webs. We also need to adapt it for a more holistic view, how each asset or concern interacts with others – in other words, assess impact on *overall* effectiveness. And we need to enhance the methodology, using iterative reviews with qualitative / quantitative scores, and 'before and after' comparison of reviews and scores.

The revision as SCORE addresses all of these concerns.

SCORE process

SCORE addresses those requirements with a SWOT-like checklist as a framework for strategy:

- *Strengths / services / support*: what we already have – existing capabilities and resources, potential for synergies
- *Challenges / capabilities needed*: what we know we need, or need to address – 'weaknesses' indicate needed capabilities and resources
- *Options / opportunities and risks*: look at the outside world for options and opportunities – opportunity is also risk, risk is also opportunity
- *Responses / returns / rewards*: probable responses of the outside world to the chosen strategy – probable or emergent consequences of action or inaction
- *Effectiveness*: probable impacts of the strategy on overall effectiveness – efficient, reliable, elegant, appropriate, integrated

Where this differs from SWOT is that we do this iteratively and recursively, comparing each dimension against the others; and we look for and record anything that can be measured, so we can assess the success of the strategy in future.

The questions for the **Strengths** dimension are much the same as for SWOT, except that we need to look both inside *and* outside our own organisation for shared strengths and support:

- *Strengths*: What would we regard as our strengths in this?
- *Services*: What services and capabilities do we have? What services can we call on from others?
- *Support*: What support-resources do we have available to us? What support do we have, from others?

The work of projects is carried out through services and capabilities, so these questions also help to identify the existing components of a 'service-oriented architecture' for the enterprise.

The subsidiary questions about support are essential. Without explicit support from senior management, the project can only be run as a concealed 'skunk-works' project – which would mean a lot more work overall, for everyone.

From here we gain both an inventory of strengths and services, and a list of probable partners in the project – in other words, what we have available to respond to opportunities, and to support the change-roadmap.

The questions for the **Challenges** dimension are again similar to SWOT. But we avoid SWOT's pejorative term 'weakness' here, instead concentrating much more on gap-analysis – on identifying what would be needed in order to achieve the key success criteria for the project:

- *Challenges*: What are the issues we need to address, within the organisation, and in relationships with partners, suppliers, other stakeholders?
- *Capabilities needed*: What new capabilities and services would we need? What skills would be required? What would be needed to develop these skills and services?

The end-result of this direction of questioning is a list of internal project-risks, and also of needed capabilities – and hence core content for a roadmap for change.

Opportunities give rise to **Options**, which in turn provide the formal basis for a 'roadmap' for change:

- *Opportunities*: What opportunities present themselves? What risks arise from with those opportunities? What opportunities arise from apparent risks?
- *Options*: What are our options in relation to those opportunities and risks? How can we act on those options? How should we prioritise those options and actions?

As with SWOT, we should be looking mostly outward here, at the 'outside' world – potential customers, partners, providers and the like.

But unlike SWOT, we always assess opportunities and risks *together*, because each is the flipside of the other: opportunities bring concomitant risks, and risks (SWOT's 'threats') also always present opportunities.

What we're looking at here – and looking *for* – are the drivers for business change: the opportunities and risks, and our options to respond to each. This identifies the *reasons* for the changes that we need to make, the priorities for the change-roadmap, and external project-risks arising directly from those opportunities.

Where 'Opportunities' is about how we look at the outside world, the **Responses** questions are more about how the outside world impinges on us:

- *Responses*: What responses would we expect from other stakeholders? from customers? competitors? providers? partners?
- *Regulations*: What regulations might arise in response to our strategy? What would be the impacts of new or upcoming legislation?
- *Returns / rewards*: What is the business value of each opportunity and risk?

Even a brief focus on regulation and legislation also helps to expand our awareness of longer-term impacts – legislation may move at a much slower pace than business cycles, for example, but its impacts cannot be avoided forever!

At least some of these expected responses should be measurable, identifying the overall returns or rewards – in other words, the business case (if any) for the strategy, and the external risks impinging indirectly on the opportunities.

The **Effectiveness** questions are the key difference from conventional SWOT analysis:

- *Efficient*: Does it optimise use of resources, minimise wastage of resources?
- *Reliable*: Is it predictable, consistent, self-correcting?
- *Elegant*: Does it have clarity, simplicity, consistency? Is it self-adjusting for human factors?

- *Appropriate*: Does it support and maximise support for business purpose?
- *Integrated*: Does it create, support and maximise synergy across all systems?

This identifies how well the 'as-is' and 'to-be' systems fit in with everything else. The aim here is to resolve a classic business dilemma: how to ensure that improvements in efficiency in one area do not cause greater inefficiencies elsewhere – a common result of traditional analysis techniques.

Working with the above questions, the steps of the SCORE methodology are as follows:

1. Select an issue
2. Start the SCORE checklist anywhere, on any dimension (often start with Strengths, or Options, but it's not required)
3. Work through all dimensions in the list (repeat and iterate in any order)
4. Assess impact of each item on effectiveness
5. Identify and record any measurable items such as new capabilities, and compare against previous SCORE assessments

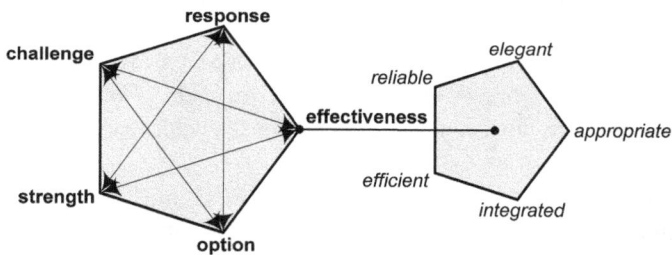

Visual representation of the SCORE methodology

Once we select an issue to assess, we can start from any dimension. We then work through all of the SCORE dimensions, using the viewpoint of each dimension as a perspective on each of the other dimensions.

And for everything that we identify, we always look at its impact on overall effectiveness, using the effectiveness-checklist: efficient, reliable, elegant, appropriate, integrated.

We also keep an eye open for anything that can be measured, whether as a numeric value or qualitatively – for example, a new capability that didn't exist at the time of a previous SCORE assessment. The reason for this is simple: it's a lot easier to manage things that can be measured.

At the end of the SCORE assessment, these are the kinds of documents we would expect to have to hand, to guide subsequent change:

- *'Strengths' dimension*: capabilities / services inventory, support / partner-map
- *'Challenges' dimension*: prioritised requirements and roadmap for change, risks / issues register
- *'Options' dimension*: strategy scenarios, opportunity / risk trade-off register
- *'Responses' dimension*: business case(s), risk-management scenarios
- *'Effectiveness' dimension*: project impact / integration assessments

To summarise, SCORE extends SWOT analysis with a new emphasis on overall *effectiveness*.. Where SWOT is a single pass through the checklist, SCORE is iterative: we repeat the process as required, to address all issues and side-themes. At the end of the process, the documents produced should provide us with a clear roadmap for business change.

SCORE in practice – a real-world example

This real example of SCORE analysis was on data-architecture strategy for a major utilities company. I've used a fictitious name for the company ('Energy'), and changed a few other identifying details, but otherwise the information here is the same as in the slides prepared for the company's enterprise-architecture group.

As you'll see, the main difference from SWOT is that the end-result is not just a go/no-go decision, but a detailed roadmap of the required changes.

Strengths...

These were Energy's existing strengths in data-architecture:

- Business support for enterprise architecture
  - higher-than-usual awareness of value of architecture

- evidence of high-level commitment
  - integrated view of the business
- Higher-level maturity of conceptual frames
  - awareness that enterprise architecture is more than IT
- Some essential work already done
  - Architecture Principles, Blueprint, BIM, Evolution SOA
- Commitment and energy!

Challenges...

These were the challenges that needed to be addressed:

- Support exists, but still under-resourced
- No adequate commercial toolsets available for business-information
  - most tools are for logical $\leftrightarrow$ physical mapping only – e.g. ERwin, Visio UML
  - System Architect probably the best of breed, but still has severe limitations – e.g. fragility of Choices list, 'user-hostile' interface etc
- Need to break free of IT-centric view
  - 'business' is too easily viewed as 'anything not-IT'

Opportunities / risks / trade-offs...

These were the opportunities, risks and trade-offs – where data-architecture fitted within the broader picture of company strategy:

- Opportunity for improved communication
  - synergies where business and IT are 'on the same page'
- Risks of market / regulatory change
  - data-architecture supports agility to external change
- Trade-off between modelling everything versus getting things done
  - improved self-knowledge and reduced long-term costs, versus project delays and loss of business credibility
  - "doing it at all takes priority over doing it right..."
  - complexity of modelling a *dynamic* world
    - the world is not static, there is no final 'future *state*'

Returns / rewards...

This was a brief summary of the kind of returns and responses from implementing (or *not* implementing) a disciplined data architecture:

- Leverage available from synergies
  - across systems
  - across products and product-lines
  - across organisational units and groups
  - across 'value-webs' with partners, suppliers etc
- Agility from Energy's increased 'self-knowledge'
  - improved ability to service new markets
  - improved ability to respond to regulatory change
  - improved ability to manoeuvre in competitive market
- Also need for increased business / technical awareness of costs of *not* doing this well...

...and effectiveness

And an overview of the impact on overall effectiveness of the current state of data-architecture in the company:

- Efficient?
  - fragmented legacy systems, too much exception-handling
- Reliable?
  - fragile data-flows, especially round-trip overwrites
  - inconsistent naming etc creates misunderstanding / rework
- Elegant?
  - market-specific models, high dependence on human processes
- Appropriate?
  - poor integration of legacy systems limits business agility
  - inadequate support for e.g. customer-centric view of data
- Integrated?
  - lack of integration identified as a key business issue
  - Evolution Initiative role is to improve overall integration

Where are the gaps?

The previous questions pointed either directly or indirectly to several strategic gaps:

- Further work needed on governance framework
  - audit-trails, owners, asset-management
- Lack of common language / translations
  - Information Model addresses this at higher level only
  - need to promote data-naming standards in business context as well as IT
  - need for common repository / 'translation' facilities
    - example: 'Jargon Buster' intranet section
- Limited awareness of *long-term* knowledge management

  "How much does it cost an organisation to forget what key employees know, to be unable to answer customer questions quickly or at all, or to make poor decisions based on faulty knowledge?"

  (Tom Davenport, director, Information Management Program, University of Texas at Austin)

- Limited awareness of non-IT data
  - integration occurs in haphazard fashion in processes
  - no systematic processes to ensure maintenance of non-IT data (e.g. narrative-knowledge techniques)
    - capabilities do exist through organisational culture

The capabilities we need (roadmap)

The gaps pointed in turn to this list of the capabilities required to fill those gaps:

- Strategic approach to data management
- Consistent governance of data and information
- Consistent handling of names and translations
- Long-term knowledge-management
  - everything changes over time: what must be preserved?
  - accuracy, relevance, security, migration, refresh, re-use
- Extend Service Oriented Architecture beyond IT
  - process as service: full integration with business process
- Integrate support for human knowledge
  - human knowledge provides *use* and *meaning* of information

Capabilities #1: strategic approach to data management

The remaining slides in the original presentation described the required capabilities in a little more detail, starting with data as a strategic asset:

- Extend concept of information / data as asset
  - Architecture Principles already established
  - Architecture Charter already established
- Establish means for costing data as asset
  - e.g. equivalents of capitalisation, depreciation etc

Capabilities #2: consistent governance of data and information

The next item was the need for consistent governance:

- Identify information / data owners at each level
  - Business Strategy
  - Business Summary
  - Logical
  - Technical
  - Transaction
- Establish cross-level review forums for all subject-areas
- Establish systematic exit-interviews for all staff and contractors in information / data-owner roles
  - capture tacit-knowledge on information / data and its use

Capabilities #3: consistent handling of names and translations

Next was the need to develop and maintain a common language, to support communication across the whole enterprise:

- Establish naming standards
  - existing standards include Information Model, Service Naming, Data Naming
  - extend these standards towards business usage
- Resolve nomenclature clashes, such as:
  - Customer vs Consumer vs Account
  - Supply Point vs Market ID
  - Location vs Supply Point Address vs Mailing Address
- Establish 'Jargon Buster' tool
  - reduces 'acronym blur', leverages / shares local knowledge, aids inter-group translation

- place on intranet (e.g. below 'find a colleague') with simple search-box
- 'anyone can post new entry' – reduces effort, increases staff engagement
  - manage as per moderated forum – moderator filters / reviews suggested entries

Capabilities #4: long-term knowledge-management

Next was a focus on management of data, information and knowledge in the *long-term* rather than only in the short-term:

- Integrated approach to whole-of-life management of data
  - *Content*: establish clear distinctions and roles for raw data, metadata and connections between data-items
  - *Accuracy*: establish governance for cleanse, de-duplication etc - regular continuous processes, not a 'once-off project'!
  - *Data safety*: identify and protect the 'single source of truth' for each data-item
  - *Sharing*: establish governance of 'need to know, need to use' security
  - *Review*: establish governance for regular reviews of data relevance ("who uses this data? in what reports? for what purpose? who *uses* those reports?")
  - *Re-use*: establish reviews / governance for re-purpose and re-use of data
  - *Lifetime*: establish real data-lifetimes, including processes for planned migration / maintenance where these exceed system lifetimes (which they often will)
- Explore how all of these issues change over medium- to long-term
  - over time, *everything* changes: plan for this!

Capabilities #5: extend Service Oriented Architecture beyond IT

Next was a need to break free from an IT-centric mindset, by promoting a broader understanding of 'service oriented architecture' across the whole enterprise:

- Service-oriented approach to process modelling
  - clarifies potential for process re-engineering
  - identifies potential process / resource re-use

- increases resilience of response in event of IT-system failure
- Establish symmetric process / data modelling
  - data as service to process, process as service to data
    - example: data / resource 'services' in BPMN (Business Process Modelling Notation) and BPEL (Business Process Execution Language) process-models
  - this type of cross-domain integration helps to improve business take-up of enterprise-architecture concepts

Capabilities #6: integrate support for human knowledge

And finally a reminder that the meaning of business information comes from people, not machines – so we need to provide support for people to derive and share that meaning:

- Establish stronger awareness that IT-stored data is only one subset of overall organisational knowledge
- Provide active support for capture and sharing of people-based 'tacit knowledge'
  - wikis and other online forums
    - already in use in some Energy development-groups
  - 'who knows what' knowledge-bases
    - see *Learning to Fly*, Collison & Parcell
  - communities of practice
    - see *Cultivating Communities of Practice*, Wenger et al.
  - sense-making and narrative-knowledge
    - see Cognitive Edge (www.cognitive-edge.com) and Anecdote Pty Ltd (www.anecdote.com.au)

Using SWOT and SCORE

Ideally, we should replace SWOT entirely with SCORE: it's more versatile, and has a much stronger emphasis on effectiveness. But it does take more time than a SWOT, and in many cases requires a better grasp of the enterprise as a whole – a broader awareness which may not be available, whether we need it or not.

So it is also possible to use SWOT and SCORE together: accept SWOT's limitations, and use it where appropriate – but *only* where appropriate. For example, use SWOT if:

- speed and simplicity have a high priority

47

- the context of the strategic issue has only narrow scope and a relatively short time-frame
- in a complex context, the chosen solution will be applied within known 'safe-fail' bounds

Use SCORE in place of SWOT if:

- the impact of the issue will cross boundaries between domains and 'silos'
- the issue has a longer time-frame – especially if measured in months or years
- overall effectiveness has a high priority
- in a complex context, there is no clear 'safe-fail'

In short, SCORE is a valuable tool, but it's not a panacea – it's just one method amongst many in the management toolkit. Used well, though, and used appropriately, you're likely to find it one of the most versatile techniques for enhancing enterprise effectiveness.

SEMPER

Overview

There's an old saying in business that "if you can't measure it, you can't manage it". Whilst that's not entirely true, there's no doubt that having *some* kind of metric usually makes management much easier. The catch is that most conventional metrics such as financial performance, return on investment, productivity, error rates and customer-satisfaction indices are all *lag-indicators*, or measurements of *past* performance. Using those metrics alone is like trying to drive the enterprise by looking in the rear-view mirror.

Instead, what we need most for management are *lead-indicators*, describing the structural elements that drive *future* performance. The SEMPER metric combines the themes of the previous chapters – the dimensions of effectiveness and relevance, and how they interact with each other – as a simple method to measure the available 'ability to do work' in the enterprise. In effect, SEMPER measures integration and performance at the innerstructure level, describing the productive capability of the entire enterprise. This provides us with a real-time 'dashboard' that tells us where the enterprise is going – not just where it's been.

This in turn points to interventions which, although they usually apply to specific and localised issues, still always act on the enterprise *as a whole*. So whilst the conventional metrics will always be important, and useful in their own ways in the right context, the picture provided by a SEMPER assessment may well be the only one that really matters.

Principles

The core idea in SEMPER is that a measure of 'ability to do work' is the key lead-indicator for enterprise capability, and hence for future performance as measured by conventional lag-indicators such as profit and the like. We measure that 'ability to do work' in different dimensions of the enterprise, and also measure how well these different dimensions support each other, as an indicator of enterprise effectiveness.

The term SEMPER acronym itself comes from the six core themes that need to be addressed in working with an organisation's inner-structure:

- Spiritual or aspirational assets – issues such as morale, culture, identity and purpose
- Emotional or relational assets – issues such as reputation, values, relationships and brands
- Mental or conceptual assets – issues such as enterprise knowledge, intellectual property and innovation
- Physical or behavioural assets – issues such as skills, resources and work-environment
- Effectiveness – issues such as efficiency, reliability, focus and direction
- Relevance – issues such as scale, perspective, scope and balance

> If the term 'spiritual' seems uncomfortable in a business context (see p.9), use the alternative reverse-acronym for SEMPER: System Effectiveness Map for Process Evaluation and Review.
>
> 'Semper' is also the Latin word for 'always' – a reminder that these themes underpin everything that the enterprise is and does.

In the simpler SEMPER-5 variant of the diagnostic – see *SEMPER-5* (p.69) - we use the five domains of the 5Ps framework – see *Five Elements* (p.19). In the full SEMPER-11 version – see *SEMPER-11* (p.95) – we derive the dimensions from the four axes and six link-themes of the tetradian, with an extra domain to measure integration across the whole – see *The dimensions of the enterprise* (p8).

We cross-reference each of these domains, recursively, with the dimensions of effectiveness – see *Effectiveness acronyms – REAL and LEARN* (p.11). This gives us a set of twenty-five subdomains in SEMPER-5, or fifty-five in SEMPER-11, within which we could assess 'ability to do work'.

And in both SEMPER variants, but in SEMPER-11 especially, we use the R^5 principles from systems-theory – see *Reviewing relevance* (p.15) – to assess how each facet of the enterprise links in with the whole.

After assessment we look at intervention-design. In both SEMPER variants, each domain and subdomain is mapped to known techniques or models that address the respective issues – see 'Assessment and interventions' in *SEMPER-5* (p. 72) and 'Assessment and interventions' in *SEMPER-11* (p.95). But we don't have to start from the 'problem area': we can, in principle, start anywhere.

This is another factor that distinguishes SEMPER from most conventional consultancy models. By its nature, integration can start anywhere, in any domain, and expand outward from there.

> Unfortunately, the same is also true of *disintegration* – which is why any 'red flag' issues identified in a SEMPER assessment need to be addressed as a matter of urgency.

This 'start anywhere' principle makes it possible to avoid a common danger with intervention design, in that tackling a major 'problem' head-on may easily inflame the issues instead, either making a difficult situation worse, or causing serious consequences elsewhere in the enterprise. With the start-anywhere principle, it's possible instead to find a related issue that's close to the known problem, and leverage the strengths in that domain to resolve the problem-issues in a more gentle and indirect way. The tetradian's dimensions and link-themes also form pathways that can suggest alternative routes to the same end.

> A real-world example. In one of our engagements, in an organisation going through a period of unexpected expansion, the SEMPER assessment identified warning-signs of dwindling standards of service, and breakdown of the staff into feuding 'tribes' – in other words issues in the SEMPER-11 domains of responsibility and relationship. There was also an opportunistic attitude to strategy – bringing short-term benefits but creating difficulties elsewhere – which pointed to potential flaws in the domain of sense-making and foresight.
>
> On the plus side, the assessment showed that there were real strengths in some aspects of leadership-by-example, and in demonstrated commitment to enterprise values.
>
> The 'start anywhere' principle suggested a two-pronged approach to the problems:
>
> - using values to move up into the aspirational domain, to recreate and reinforce an intentionally inclusive sense of organisational identity that could unify the 'tribes'; and
> - developing and supporting an emphasis on personal leadership as a source of personal pride in work.
>
> An Open Space event involving staff from all levels and all business-units – in other words focussing on narrative and dialogue as a bridge between relations and knowledge – also helped to resolve the strategy issues, and created a new sense of engagement throughout the enterprise.

It worked well – very well. A year later, that organisation became the market leader in its field, and has remained there ever since – though we can't claim *all* of the credit for that, of course!

The advantage of SEMPER and the start-anywhere principle is that it provides a consistent framework to manage this complexity, and guide the process of selecting appropriate tools and techniques. There's more detail later on how to use SEMPER for this kind of organisational transformation and development; but first, we need to explore how to use SEMPER for assessing overall effectiveness.

Assessment

Assessment can be carried out using either of the two current variants: SEMPER-5 and SEMPER-11.

SEMPER-5 – see *SEMPER-5*, p.69 – is a simpler variant for quick assessments and for more general use. Based on the Five Elements version of the framework, and with a simplified scoring system, it can be used with only minimal training – the material in this book should suffice as a start. By mapping between Five Elements and the full tetradian, results from SEMPER-5 assessments are upwards-compatible: in the software-based versions, SEMPER-5 data-sets can be imported direct into a SEMPER-11 data-set.

SEMPER-11 – see *SEMPER-11*, p.95 – is a more advanced variant based on the full tetradian version of the framework. It's best used by experienced consultants, as the scoring system requires a good understanding of systems-theory and organisational complexity. But it does provide a richer mapping between domains and actions, to support more precise targeting of interventions. The inclusion of the tetradian link-themes in the assessment also permits a broader range of choices for alternative interventions in the more difficult cases – those with many low '1'- or '2'-type scores.

The overall SEMPER framework is language-independent, and largely culture-independent, but may be too abstract for general use on its own. Both SEMPER-11 and SEMPER-5 simplify this by using a cue-phrase to describe each pairing of domain and effectiveness category. SEMPER-5 simplifies scoring still further with a set of descriptive phrases or 'word-pictures' that typify each score-level in each domain and category.

Ideally, the cue-phrases and 'word-pictures' should be derived by narrative techniques from within the enterprise itself, reflecting its own unique language and culture. However, the default phrase-sets used in this book should be adequate for basic use in most English-speaking cultures.

The purpose of the cue-phrases and (in SEMPER-11) assessment-questions for each domain, and the generic relevance-questions that apply to all domains, is to evoke a deeper understanding of the issues in the respective context, and how they affect the effectiveness and integration of the whole.

In practice, though, the questions may sometimes not work well straight from the page. For example, a cue-phrase such as "How are the boundaries of 'We' maintained?" makes sense within the SEMPER framework, but to many people it might at first seem meaningless. So with SEMPER-11 especially, it may be necessary to translate a cue-phrase into terms that make more sense within the context. For example, "What do you do to make sure that new people fit in with the way you do things here?", or "What help do you get to stand your ground if you're being pressured by a business partner to take part in a dodgy deal?" – and weave it into an ordinary conversation about more everyday matters.

Both variants provide background information and questions to support the assessment. Both allow the assessment to be carried out in any sequence as appropriate, whilst still ensuring that all domains of the assessment are evaluated. And both variants are each available in a manual format – see *SEMPER-5 assessment*, p.84 and *SEMPER-11 assessment*, p.115 – or as an internet or intranet application – see, for example, www.sempermetrics.com.

As a consultancy tool, SEMPER can be used to guide both assessment and intervention. It can be applied iteratively over any period of time, in any appropriate sequence, to any required depth. The basic SEMPER process is as follows:

1. Select an initial SEMPER domain to assess – either an issue chosen by the client or indicated in preliminary discussion, or the default of 'Aspirations'.

2. Explore the issues in that theme, using the questions indicated for the domain.

3. Use the LEARN keywords (elegant, efficient, appropriate, reliable, integrated) to evaluate effectiveness in the context.

4. Use the R^5 principles (recursion, rotation, reflexion, reciprocation, resonance) to explore the issues in greater depth, and to assess their integration with the whole.

5. Assign a 1-5 score to each pairing of domain and effectiveness-category, with an optional adjustment (+1 for improving, 0 for stable, -1 for worsening) to indicate probable future trends for each.

6. Select another domain, either from the sequence shown on the paper form or in the software application, or by following any of the trails to related dimensions, link-themes or overall integration.

7. Repeat until all appropriate issues in all domains have been addressed.

The same iterative process is used for assessment and for intervention design. In practice, a SEMPER assessment is also a kind of intervention, as the act of assessment and evaluation itself brings issues to light and provides pointers towards their resolution.

The end-result of the assessment for a domain is a set of scores on a 1-5 scale (see *Scoring an assessment* below), each matched to the respective cue-phrase. This provides a visual summary of effectiveness issues throughout the whole context, and a data-set that can be aggregated and re-used in many different ways.

The basic tabular summary lists the results for the assessment in a standard report-layout, optionally including any comments and trends as well as the basic score for each assessment-statement. Since SEMPER covers every aspect of the innerstructure, including its overall integration, the summary provides a literal 'balanced scorecard' for the context. In the software-based versions, the evaluations are colour-coded, so that any '1' or '2' scores are immediately visible as 'red-flag' issues – 'deal-killers' that put the whole enterprise at risk and need urgent attention.

The software versions also provide an alternative single-page 'dashboard' view of the assessment, laid out in grid form, with domains providing one axis and the effectiveness-keywords the other axis. An optional second grid shows the future results predicted by the recorded trends, providing an immediate visual comparison of the organisation's trends.

Scoring an assessment

The scoring system used in all SEMPER variants is based on a power-model that highlights a key dichotomy about power and work: in physics, power is defined as 'the ability to do work', whereas in many social contexts power is essentially defined as 'the ability to *avoid* work', or to entrap others into doing the respective work. The social definition is dysfunctional or 'power-against', as it creates a negative resonance towards a 'lose/lose' – usually seen either as the illusory 'win/lose' or the less-common 'lose/win' – from which eventually everyone loses. By contrast, the physics definition is functional or 'power-with', in that it supports positive resonance leading towards a 'win/win' from which everyone gains. (See the glossary in *Appendix A: Glossary*, p.127, for more details on these terms.)

For convenience, the SEMPER scoring system places this range from strong negative resonance to strong positive on a simple 1-5 scale, as summarised below:

5: Excellent (full-scope effective)

Summary: systematic, conscious, context-aware use of emergent / collective techniques, self-propagating and linking with other domains *[the ideal as a 'start anywhere' area]*

Power-themes: power-from-within to power-with – individual to collective

Competence category: unconscious-competence

Commitment: wholeness-responsibility

Decision-style: co-creating

Scoring suggestions: assign a '5' when this aspect is not only well supported, but it either helps the integration of other domains, or can be used as an example in developing other domains or in other effectiveness-categories in the same domain.

- a '5' score will typically occur only in some aspects of some domains: for example, a strong focus on customer service enhancing quality and personal responsibility throughout the whole organisation, or a well-established 'credo' defining the organisation's vision and values.

4: Good (local effective)

Summary: includes use of emergent / collective techniques such as self-organised teams, scenarios, diversity and the like, but often in a fragmentary way, not integrated with other domains, and often without a theoretical framework to link it to others *[may be used as an example / leverage if no '5' is available]*

Power-themes: power-with to power-from-within – collective to individual

Competence category: conscious-competence

Commitment: functional diversity

Decision-style: consulting

Scoring suggestions: assign a '4' when this aspect is working well, but could probably do with further improvement at some stage, especially in links to other domains.

- a '4' score will be more common than a '5', and would be typical for most aspects of high-performing organisations and for the best aspects of average ones.

3: Acceptable (efficient)

Summary: efficient up to the limit of analytic / predictable – the benchmark or Best Practice level – but often applied without much awareness of the broader context *[stable, but could be improved]*

Power-themes: power-neutral – dysfunction is counterbalanced by functional power

Competence category: plateau of control

Commitment: 'best practice'

Decision-style: testing

Scoring suggestions: assign a '3' when this aspect is neither a hindrance nor much of a help, though attention to improve it would probably be described as 'important but not urgent'.

- a '3' score is typical for most domains in average-performing organisations: good enough to get by but not capable on its own of supporting stellar performance. Quite often, though, careful attention on just one or two of these '3' issues will be enough to lift the entire organisation to a whole new order of performance and effectiveness.

2: Below needs (passive dysfunction)

Summary: should be efficient in the local context, but will create imbalance passively due to lack of integration with other areas *[needs to be addressed to prevent decline]*

Power-themes: power-under – evasion of responsibility

Competence category: conscious-incompetence

Commitment: compartments / silos

Decision-style: selling

Scoring suggestions: assign a '2' when weakness in this aspect of the domain is having significant impact on overall effectiveness, and needs attention as soon as practicable to prevent a downward spiral.

- a '2' score usually arises from too narrow a focus, and lack of awareness of the impact of local actions on the workings of the whole – the classic effect of over-specialisation and poor support for generalists, resulting in disconnected 'silos' and private fiefdoms.
- all '2' scores should be flagged as 'significant' issues in the assessment-summary, and need to be resolved before overall effectiveness can be improved.

1: Poor (active dysfunction)

Summary: evidence of serious power-problems – some aspect actively creating imbalance, and 'infecting' other domains *[placing organisation at risk – needs urgent attention*

Power-themes: power-over – self over others

Competence category: unconscious-incompetence

Commitment: fragmentation

Decision-style: telling

Scoring suggestions: assign a '1' when weakness in this area is not only causing serious damage to overall effectiveness, but is 'infecting' other aspects of the domain or other domains, and needs urgent attention to resolve.

- a '1' score usually arises from some form of power imbalance deep within the organisation's innerstructure. Such issues place the entire enterprise at risk, and are the most common cause of organisational failure: classic examples include mismatch between espoused and actual values, a predatory attitude to customers, employees and other stakeholders, complacency and 'groupthink' as a substitute for strategic foresight, or even basic management issues such as poor cost control.

- all '1' scores should be flagged as 'serious' issues in the assessment-summary, and will require urgent attention. However, by their nature, such issues are often denied and 'undiscussable', resulting in classic 'fire-fighting', lurching from crisis to crisis and always looking outside for something to save the day – a 'hero' manager, perhaps, or the next in an endless succession of management fads – anything, in fact, to avoid facing the deeper issues within the organisation itself. Designing and implementing successful interventions for these intractable issues will invariably prove to be the hardest part of any business-integration process.

Notes on scoring

Although the cue-phrase is different in each domain, in effect each represents a domain-specific way to express the same questions about effectiveness in the overall context:

- *Is the activity in this domain efficient?* – it maximises the return and minimises the use of energies and resources
- *Is it reliable?* – it can be relied upon to deliver the required results
- *Is it elegant?* – it supports the human factors in the domain
- *Is it appropriate?* – it supports the overall purpose and minimises distractions from that purpose
- *Is it integrated with the whole?* – it links with, supports and is supported by the other domains

For example, the aim of the cue-phrase "Identity and purpose consistently described and maintained" is to provide a way to assess whether the processes that apply to this domain – 'Aspirations', the domain of identity and purpose – can be relied upon to support and maintain identity and purpose *for the whole context.*

The generic 'Relevance' questions in SEMPER-11 aim to provide reminders about scale, perspective, balance and the like. Using the same example, this means that identity and purpose need to apply and be supported at every level, from the individual, to the work-group, the department, the business-unit and so on, and that these need to link between and support *all* levels and perspectives – not just the identity and purpose of one group of stakeholders, such as management, unions, customers, suppliers or shareholders.

In reality, every cue-phrase relates, if only in part, to issues that are intangible and all but unmeasurable. This especially applies to links between domains. Yet even if they are 'unmeasurable', it is still possible and useful to form an opinion – in other words, make a subjective yet considered assessment – about how well that aspect of the domain is working in relation to the whole. In SEMPER-5, the scoring decision is simplified by limiting the range of assessment to a 'closest match' to one of five alternative descriptions. Backed up where necessary by additional comments, this provides both a qualitative summary for the domain *and* a simple 1-5 scale that can be used for overall scores.

In SEMPER-11 especially, each assessment involves a balance of many different factors. For example, if all levels of employees are engaged in developing vision and strategy, you would probably assign a score of '3' or even a '4' for the respective cue-phrase; but you might reduce this to a '2' if there is a strong 'us versus them' attitude toward suppliers or customers, and definitely to a '1' if the only declared 'purpose' is that of 'enhancing shareholder value', as this is likely to weaken the commitment of everyone involved (with the possible exception of senior management).

If in doubt, score one level lower than your initial evaluation. This may seem pessimistic, but it counters a natural tendency towards wishful thinking, and in most cases is more realistic than scoring upwards.

Note too that the wider culture will also play an important part in the overall context, and hence needs to be taken into account in your assessment. At present, the reality is that many aspects of the mainstream economic, legal and business frameworks at local, national, regional and global levels all actively degrade enterprise effectiveness, and all but mandate organisational failure within a relatively short period. (This assertion may at first sound extreme, but it soon becomes self-evident from the broader perspective of SEMPER.) Most commercial organisations that follow a 'business-as-usual' paradigm, with its over-focus on the financial bottom line and its emphasis on efficiency over effectiveness, would be likely to score a '2' or even a '1' in several different aspects, especially in relation to aspirational themes around identity and purpose, and appropriate management and maintenance of in-tangible assets.

As a general guideline, an organisation needs to score at least a '4' in more than half of the assessment criteria, with no worse than a '2' in any area, before sustainable excellence can be achieved. That this needs to be done within a wider milieu which not only rarely supports this, but often actively works against it, is one of the most interesting challenges for present-day business leaders.

It's important to understand that the framework describes only the impact of each of these levels on overall effectiveness – not necessarily that a '5' level is always to be desired. In general, '2'- and, especially '1'-type responses are likely to cause problems, and should be minimised wherever practicable; but some compliance-areas, such as occupational health and safety, medicine and the law, will necessarily restrict personal choice and personal responsibility, and hence mandate that a '3'-type would usually be the highest achievable level in that context.

Aggregations – using multiple perspectives

A single SEMPER assessment in itself provides a useful 'dashboard' view. SEMPER's design draws out the characteristic reflexion of all complex-systems, so even a single perspective will still portray a meaningful and valid view of the whole enterprise. Yet often the greatest value comes from aggregations which combine or compare data from several different assessments. The key types of aggregations are:

- *comparison* – two or more assessment-summaries shown side by side in tabular form
- *chart* – as for comparison, but with assessment-summaries overlaid as graph-lines or as a shaded 'river diagram'
- *statistical map* – mapping across a broader set of assessments, showing minima, median/mean and maxima

Some examples of applications include:

- *comparison over time* – a dashboard used to compare assessments of the same context by quarter, year or other interval, to show changes over time
- *whole-of-organisation* – a statistical dashboard showing the overall 'effectiveness health' of the organisation across all departments and business units, highlighting any 'red flag' issues and any potential aspects to support stronger integration

- *inside/outside view* – a dashboard to compare assessments of the same context by 'insiders' and 'outsiders', used for issues such as reputation management, market alignment and construction of value webs
- *horizontal scan* – views from the same level but different functional areas within the organisation (e.g. all senior executive, or all second-level managers); highlights potential conflicts, assists in whole-of-organisation gap-analysis
- *vertical scan* – views from different levels within the same functional area; provides direct comparison of different emphases and drivers at the different levels of the organisation, even with the same nominal scope
- *spherical scan* – views from immediately above, immediately below and at same level as a single chosen context (like 360° feedback); combines horizontal and vertical scans to create an overall picture of potential issues

An advantage of using SEMPER in place of conventional 360°-feedback techniques is that it reduces the emotional loading: it describes views of a *context* rather than a person, making apparent criticism easier to accept and address.

Common statistical techniques can also be used to derive standard deviation and mean scores, though these are perhaps less directly useful than identifying specific areas of concern – especially the crucial '1'-type issues.

In general, any strong disparity between perspectives will point to potential or actual areas of conflict. Consistent low scores across most or all perspectives point to 'undiscussable' issues that will need to be addressed by indirect rather than direct tactics.

Interpretation

The SEMPER diagnostic describes a view of the whole context from one group's or person's perspective. In effect, it provides a means to quantify not just individual performance, but integration and effectiveness of the context *as a whole*. The scores in each domain and category identify key indicators of effectiveness not only within the specific area, but also in relation to the whole *as* whole. The optional trend-adjustment for the score provides an additional 'lead-indicator' for the future, identifying potential problems to be addressed or areas that can be leveraged to improve overall integration, using the key start-anywhere principle of the framework.

Overall scores

The overall score provides a useful overview of integration and the potential for further improvement:

- **20% or less** (20% is minimum-possible score before adjustment for trends): actively dysfunctional in all areas; may be beyond recovery
- **20%-30%**: severely dysfunctional (commercial organisations usually unprofitable); may be recoverable, but in danger of spiralling beyond recovery; in some cases may be recovered by 'hidden' integration techniques such as process/workflow analysis that draws out people-connections and tacit knowledge, but often recoverable only by 'shock tactics' that make the dysfunctionality plainly visible and re-emphasise a return to collective purpose
- **30%-40%**: passively dysfunctional (commercial organisations usually at break-even); often typified by excessive bureaucracy and a 'silo' mentality; can usually be improved by integration techniques that leverage successes and acknowledge yet *avoid* 'undiscussable' problem-areas
- **40%-50%**: functional bureaucracy (commercial organisations usually at peer-average performance); 'problem' areas often typified by frustration rather than cynicism and despair; can usually be improved by leveraging a single integration-theme such as quality or innovation to loosen silo-boundaries
- **50%-60%**: best-practice (commercial organisations usually in upper range of peer-average); can only be improved by loosening the command-and-control mentality and supporting individual responsibility at the rules-versus-guidelines boundary
- **60%-70%**: beyond efficiency (commercial organisations show clear distance from peers); improvements usually derived from increasing whole-of-system awareness such as recursive relationships with partners and the wider community
- **70%-80%**: effective responsibility (commercial organisations show consistent *long-term* higher-than-average performance); if achievable, improvements usually derived from emergent ethos and sense of shared destiny

- **80%-90%**: wholeness responsibility (commercial organisations show quantum performance difference from peers, but often not sustainable); emphasis usually needs to be on sustaining and maintaining rather than attempting further improvement
- **90%+**: full integration (in general, achievable only for small groups, and usually only for short periods); often desirable to create example for wider whole-of-system improvements, but inherently unstable and unsustainable; emphasis needs to be on acceptance of natural 'fallback' to sustainable lower levels when the immediate task is complete

This indicates that, for a commercial enterprise, a score in the 50%-60% range would be a good result: well below peak potential, but still relatively high by comparison with most of the organisation's peers. In practice, a 100% score is neither achievable nor, in most cases, even desirable; an overall score of around 80% would be a more realistic target, and probably more sustainable over the longer term.

As a comparison, the mean score for effectiveness at the societal level is usually around the 40%-50% level, dependent on the context. In the business domain, though, the mean may perhaps be as low as 30% or less, given the common insistence on dysfunctional forms of competition and the often extreme emphasis on short-term financial results over any kind of investment for longer-term performance.

Moving beyond those mean-levels improves performance, but also increases the tension of the natural 'pull-back' towards the mean: for example, organisations which place strong emphasis on intangibles – especially people-oriented intangibles such as morale and work/life balance – may place themselves at risk of hostile takeover by other organisations with a more predatory short-term perspective. A lack of understanding at board level of the difference between short-term efficiency and long-term effectiveness can easily destroy most of an organisation's capacity for sustainable performance, yet without showing any visible sign of damage for some months or years – a classic longer-term resonance effect in all complex-systems which conceals the real cause of many organisational problems. Sustainable high effectiveness and high performance is not easy, and for a large enterprise almost invariably depends on some kind of unifying ethos or 'creed' which provides an enduring sense of mission and purpose.

Specific scoring issues

Note that the overall score is a useful a summary, but is often less important than key scores in specific areas, and the overall range of scores. For most enterprises, a typical 'best' would consist at least one or two 5s, mostly 4s and 3s, a few 2s, and no 1s.

A '5'-type score is relatively unusual. For best performance, every enterprise needs to find at least one '5', though too many can actually make it *less* stable. Every '5' represents an area which can be leveraged to maximise effectiveness in every other area.

A '4' or a '3' represent functional areas with potential opportunities for improvement.

A '2' represents an issue that needs to be addressed.

A '1' represents active dysfunctionality which can self-propagate to infect other areas of the enterprise. '1'-scores are 'red flags': *any area showing a '1' score has the potential to destroy the entire enterprise,* and must be resolved as soon as possible. The difficulty is that any attempt to tackle '1'-type issues directly will further inflame the problems; in practice, as described later, they can be tackled safely only by working on less-inflamed areas around them.

Another key concern is the disparity of scores in different areas. High disparity will highlight common sources of 'unexpected' instability, whereas low disparity – especially where all the scores are low – often indicates potential difficulty in identifying suitable areas to leverage for improvement. Some SEMPER-5 examples:

- commercial organisations tend to be stronger in the *Preparation, Process* and *Performance* domains, but often at risk in the *People* and especially the *Purpose* domains
- government and non-profit organisations tend to be either very high in the *People* domain (or very low – indicating political problems), but are often weak in the *Process* or *Performance* domains
- academic organisations tend to over-emphasise the *Purpose* domain (nothing gets started, let alone finished) or *Preparation* domain (resulting in 'analysis paralysis')
- family organisations and other SMEs tend to have a wider overall disparity than large organisations, reflecting the greater difficulty for smaller organisations to maintain consistent awareness of everything, but in most cases also providing a wider range of opportunity to leverage higher-score areas for improved overall effectiveness

Suggested actions

The notes above summarise what the SEMPER-5 diagnostic shows about an enterprise; but what happens next? What would the results suggest we should do differently come Monday morning? In practice, this always depends on which areas are highlighted for action – either because they are weaker, or because they can be leveraged to help lift other aspects of the organisation's game.

The most powerful tools to create sustainable improvements are the large-group interventions such as Future Search and Open Space, which operate directly at the '5'-type level. However, all of them require facilitators and managers to relinquish control, agendas and outcomes, to allow requirements to emerge from the collective space. Any attempt at control – to force the process back to a more comfortable '3'-type level, or below – will not only cause failure, but may well entrench cynicism, 'change fatigue' and resistance to further interventions. For the same reason, agreements made during this type of emergent process must always be carried through to completion: if there's a risk that commitments will be withdrawn, it's best not to attempt these processes at all.

Where the problem-area is a '1'-type issue, it's best to **not** attempt to dive straight in and 'fix the problem'. '1'-type issues are often deeply entrenched and 'undiscussable', so hitting them hard – the standard approach in conventional consulting techniques – only makes things worse, often provoking a reaction far out of proportion to the event. Instead, as with an inflamed wound, it's best to tackle them gently, often by deliberately looking away elsewhere – in other words, find another area with a '3'-type or above for which the diagnostic shows a 'hook' that can link back to the inflamed area, and leverage improvement from there. In SEMPER-11 such alternate paths are shown directly via the six link-themes. With SEMPER-5, choose an area in either the same domain or same category that has a higher-level score, linking back to the inflamed area with that domain or category as the 'hook'.

For the common '2'-type problem of organisational 'silos' – "never let the left hand know what the right or middle hands are doing" – the best tactic is an emphasis on the role of the generalist. Every enterprise has people whose natural inclination is to wander from place to place, to talk, exchange ideas and stories, keep track of how things link together. Some such roles are formally recognised – project manager is one example – but most are not. These 'horizontal' connections are essential for enterprise integration and effectiveness, but in most cases are thwarted by the 'vertical' orientation of enterprise structures. The more that generalists do their real work of creating links and connections, the more they are likely to be penalised for 'failing' to perform against what are – for them – entirely the wrong types of performance metrics.

A common survival-tactic for generalists in large organisations is to shelter under the wing of a powerful patron, often assigned an indefinable title such as 'ideation manager' or 'communications analyst' that protects them from conventional performance assessments. The catch with this tactic is that it remains dependent on the whim and status of the patron: if either are lost, the protection goes with it. Far better to develop performance-metrics for generalists that are actually meaningful in practice: never an easy task, but a necessary one if the enterprise wants to move onward.

Moving beyond a '3'-type level – and especially from '4'-type to '5'-type – is not something that can often be done by incremental improvement: it requires a true quantum jump, a change from one state to an entirely different other. The '3'-type level is the best that can be achieved with conventional command-and-control; moving to the '4'-type level requires that 'control' be dropped, instead recognising the unique attributes of each individual; and moving to the '5'-type level requires that 'command' be dropped too, allowing wholeness-responsibility to arise from within each individual. This last level of trust is impractical in most organisational contexts: the few commercial organisations with sustained high '5'-type levels, such as Ricardo Semler's Semco, all operate within high-margin niche markets. But for the rest of us, no matter how tightly constrained our environment may be, it's always possible to have at least one or two '5'-type areas, and it's always something that's worth striving for: it's what makes the difference between the good and the truly great.

From assessment to action

The aim of the assessment is to identify strengths and challenges within the innerstructure, to guide intervention design and tool selection. Despite the marketing hype of some proponents, no one tool does everything, but each has its value and its place. The table below summarises the scope and limitations of a range of well-known models, books and techniques, in relation to the tetradian's ten domains.

	S	E	M	P	S-E	E-P	P-M	M-E	M-S	S-P
Models										
Quality systems - TQM, ISO-9000	°		⇔	⇔	°	°	⇔			°
Business Process Reengineering			⇔	⇔						
Knowledge Management			⇔				⇔	(⇔)	(⇔)	
Emotional Intelligence		⇔			°	⇔				
Spiritual Intelligence	⇔	°			°	°				
Books										
Seven Habits (Covey)	⇔	⇔		⇔	⇔	(⇔)	°			⇔
Liberating the Corporate Soul (Barrett)	°	⇔		°	⇔	⇔			°	
Competing for the Future (Hamel and Prahalad)			°		⇔				⇔	
Other techniques										
Coaching / mentoring	⇔	⇔		°	°	⇔	°			⇔
Large-group interventions (Open Space, World Café)	°	°	⇔	°	⇔	⇔	°	⇔	⇔	

Key: ⇔ - primary focus, main domain(s) addressed   (⇔) - primary focus available in some variants only

  ° - secondary focus (partly addressed - needs linkage to other tools for full integration)

Dimensions: S - spiritual/aspirational, E - emotional/relational, M – mental / conceptual, P - physical/behavioural

Link-themes: S-E - vision and values, E-P - leadership, P-M - active learning, M-E - narrative and dialogue, M-S - sense-making and foresight , S-P - responsibility and empowerment

Enterprise effectiveness depends on ensuring that all the inner-structure domains are fully supported in the overall operations and activities of the enterprise. As the table shows, each tool or technique focusses most of its attention on one or two domains, occasionally more. (Large-group intervention techniques such as Open Space and World Café cover the widest range of domains, but in general are only practicable as 'events' rather than everyday work-processes.) So in practice, every enterprise will need to use a variety of techniques and approaches, in different combinations as appropriate, to cover all domains.

The key to effectiveness lies in linking different and often disparate techniques together to support the whole. If this integration is not done, the result is a succession of short-term 'management fads', each introduced with high hopes and great excitement, only to fade away after a mere few months, and all too often in a welter of recrimination, blame and renewed cynicism. Lack of systematic integration is also one of the primary reasons why organisations fragment into dissociated 'silos' and fiefdoms. It's only when there's a renewed awareness of the whole *as* whole that the unnecessary boundaries start to dissolve, and stronger effectiveness becomes possible.

Interestingly, it's the secondary domains that are often most important in this, particularly in the relational domain and its link-themes, as they provide 'hooks' to attach other tools, creating a seamless integration. When these 'hooks' are absent – as in most implementations of business process reengineering – the stage is set for an almost inevitable failure. For other models, and even to some extent for BPR, the problem was more in implementation than in design: for example, key aspirational and relational themes in Deming's concept of quality management – such as the need for clear vision, and his exhortation to "drive out fear!" – were watered down in TQM, and all but lost from the earlier versions of ISO9000. It's only recently that the importance of the relational domains in sharing of tacit knowledge has been fully recognised in mainstream implementations of knowledge management.

The advantage of SEMPER here is that it does not seek to replace any existing tools and techniques; instead, it provides new ways to leverage what the organisation already knows and does. SEMPER can be used as an intervention technique in its own right, especially in the strategy and foresight area; but its main use is to provide a framework in which existing tools at last *do* make practical sense.

SEMPER-5

Overview

Use and interpretation of the full SEMPER-11 diagnostic requires specialist skills, especially in assessments for large, complex organisations. Yet there's also a clear need for a simpler metric which covers the same overall scope, but which is more closely matched to the needs and experience of general business users.

SEMPER-5 fills this gap. It is particularly appropriate as a means to collect quick 'snapshot' views of the organisation, often for re-use in aggregations such as cross-departmental 'scorecards' and 360° feedback. Assessments created with SEMPER-5 are also upwards compatible with the full SEMPER model.

> The Legal Bit: we've used SEMPER extensively for some years now, so we know it works, but we can't be liable for its use by others outside of our control. Commonsense applies: all reasonable care has been taken, but use it at your own risk etc etc. Fair enough?

Structure

To understand what SEMPER-5 describes, it's useful to review the SEMPER framework that underlies it. As we've seen, the tetradian describes the enterprise in terms of four distinct dimensions:

- *behavioural* or physical – the facilities and capabilities of the enterprise, and actions and experiences of individual people
- *conceptual* or mental – the shared knowledge, beliefs and systems of the enterprise, and the knowledge and ideas of individual people
- *relational* or emotional – the shared relationships of the enterprise within itself and with its outside stakeholders and other organisations, and the relationships and interactions of individual people
- *aspirational* or spiritual – shared and personal aspirations, vision, values, purpose and culture across the enterprise

There is also a hidden 'fifth dimension', the process of *integration* which links those four dimensions into a unified whole.

SEMPER-11 provides an assessment in each of these domains, and also in each of the six link-themes that act as the 'bridges' between each pair of the four dimensions – for example, *active learning*, which bridges the behavioural and conceptual dimensions. For simplicity, SEMPER-5 follows the Five Elements structure (see p.19): it merges the tetradian link-themes into the base domains, and uses a slightly different mapping of dimensions that is easier to match to common organisational structures. This is summarised in the following table.

Domain	Tagline	Tetradian dimension	Time-focus
Purpose	"vision, values, purpose, identity"	Spiritual / Aspirational	mid- to far-future
People	"quality of internal and external relationships, trust	Emotional / Relational	range from far past to far future
Preparation	"knowledge, planning, mindsets, beliefs"	forward-view component of Mental / Conceptual	near future
Process	"resources, actions, environments"	Physical / Practical	now!
Performance	"completions, closing the loops"	rearward-view component of Mental / Conceptual	past

SEMPER-5 domains

In principle, through reflexion, every domain occurs in every part and every level of the organisation. In practice, though, different organisational functions tend to emphasise specific domains:

- *purpose*: emphasised in strategy, research and development, and some aspects of marketing
- *people*: emphasised in personnel/human resources, marketing and public relations
- *preparation*: emphasised in business development, planning, scheduling, distribution, training and performance-support systems
- *process*: emphasised in manufacture, production and sales
- *performance*: emphasised in sales-fulfilment, accounts, record-keeping, performance measures

In each case, the respective business-functions need to score high in their 'preferred' SEMPER-5 domains, since they are in effect 'holding the flag' for that domain on behalf of the organisation. (If not, this is in itself a clear source of problems for the organisation.) Any other domains that are scored high provide useful 'hooks' to support closer integration with the related business functions.

Integration-functions such as quality, IT, OH&S, logistics, facilities and infrastructure need (though are rarely allowed) a near-equal emphasis on all five domains.

For each domain, the SEMPER-5 diagnostic presents a set of cue-phrases which form the framework for the scoring. The statements are split into five categories, which map recursively to the original SEMPER dimensions. The domains provide a function oriented perspective, whilst the categories describe how those same themes tend to be expressed in practice *within* a single function.

The effectiveness categories thus provide *an alternate view of the same issues*, seen from a different perspective. The mapping is not as precise in SEMPER-5 as it is in SEMPER-11, but still delivers a similar result: a kind of self-reflecting 360° feedback on the context as a whole.

Category	Tagline	Associated domain
Efficient	"makes best use of energies and resources"	Preparation / Performance [conceptual]
Reliable	"delivers expected results consistently and sustainably"	Process [physical]
Elegant	"supports the human elements within the context"	People [relational]
Appropriate	"supports and is aligned to the overall purpose"	Purpose [aspirational]
Integrated	"linked to, supports and supported by all other domains"	(integration) ['soul' of the enterprise]

SEMPER-5 effectiveness categories

Significant disparity between the two perspectives – categories within domains, or domains within categories – implies the same kind of warning as for disparity within a single perspective. For example, all low-scores in one category, such as 'Appropriate', indicates the same kind of problems as for low scores in the matching 'Purpose' domain. Conversely, higher scores in one category (in a commercial organisation, often 'Efficient' or 'Reliable') in an otherwise low-scored domain can act as 'hooks' into the matching domain (in this example, either 'Preparation' / 'Performance' or 'Process' respectively), providing opportunities to leverage existing successes and competencies in lower-scoring domains. For examples of how to put this into practice, see 'Suggested actions' in *SEMPER* (p.65).

Assessment and interventions

The following notes summarise assessment and suggested intervention techniques for each 'cell' – pairing of domain and category – in SEMPER-5. The matching tetradian link-theme is shown in brackets after the cell-name; note that link-themes may apply to several cells, or be split across different cells.

To conduct the assessment, select an appropriate starting cell, dependent on the key issue or problem. (For general overviews, start at the beginning of the 5Ps cycle, with the 'Purpose/Efficient' cell.) Then:

1. using the cell's cue-phrase and the respective notes below as a guide, review the selected context; in particular, note the phrases and other language that people tend to use in describing their experience of that context

2. from the example descriptions provided for the cell, select the phrase which most closely matches the 'flavour' within that context; mark the respective score appropriately on the diagnostic
   [on the paper form, circle the respective score; on the online version, select the descriptive phrase from the dropdown list]

3. optionally, assign a trend-adjustment for each score: +1 for improving, 0 for stable, or -1 for worsening
   [on the paper form, write the respective trend-adjustment; on the online version, select the trend-value from the dropdown list]

4. move to the next cell, following the sequence of domains or categories as appropriate

Repeat this sequence until all cells have been assessed.

See *SEMPER-5 assessment* (p.84) for a set of example forms that can be used for SEMPER-5 assessments.

Purpose - vision, values, purpose and identity

Themes: identity, morale, brand awareness

Purpose / Efficient *(Strategy)*

Cue-phrase: "Vision, values and purpose are clear, simple and easy to apply in practice"

Summary: "Vision provides direction and inspiration for daily activities": look at support for direction and purpose, and assets such as morale and collective identity, staff turnover and how vision is applied in practice; also for keywords in the language used by members to describe the organisation and what they stand for.

Scoring issues: Score high for clear boundaries between rules / compliance versus principles for autonomous decision-making; score low for 'fire-fighting', lack of focus, or mismatch between espoused and actual values.

Typical intervention models and techniques:
 • vision/values as 'credo' for decision-making

Purpose / Reliable *(Commitment)*

Cue-phrase: "Vision, values and purpose provide clear guidelines to manage change"

Summary: "Direction, purpose and identity provide a reliable anchor to guide response to change": look for principle-based decision-making, symbols of identity, and long-term view – for example, that decisions for change are linked to vision and values.

Scoring issues: Score high where identity and purpose seem inherent in daily activities and thinking; score low for any tendency to treat aspirational assets (e.g. morale) as physical.

Typical intervention models and techniques:
 • emphasis on principles with rules as default

Purpose / Elegant *(Vision and values)*

Cue-phrase: "Vision, values and purpose inspire personal commitment by members"

Summary: "Purpose gives a feeling of belonging and self-worth": look for collective sense of identity, unity, common purpose, especially where expressed in emotive and inclusive terms.

Scoring issues: Score high for enthusiasm and commitment; score low for evidence of cynicism and disaffection, indifference or fragmentation into warring 'tribes'.

Typical intervention models and techniques:

- use of emotive language to enhance engagement

Purpose / Appropriate *(Power/Property/Responsibility)*

Cue-phrase: "Vision, values and purpose include social, environmental and global concerns"

Summary: "Purpose supports relationships at every level": look for consistent principles that guide partnerships within the enterprise, with suppliers and business-partners, with customers and investors, with local communities and advocacy groups, and 'global citizenship'; also for awareness of environmental impact and the 'long view'.

Scoring issues: Score high for wide-scope awareness and consistency of principles across layers; score low for inwardly-focussed / physical-only orientation.

Typical intervention models and techniques:

- explicit reference to 'outside' contexts (vision / role / mission / goals layering)
- whole-of-context standards – ISO-14000, ISO-17000, etc

Purpose / Integrated *(Foresight)*

Cue-phrase: "Vision, values and purpose anchor all aspects of the enterprise"

Summary: "Purpose and identity bring everything together": look for evidence that values and identity guide awareness of the whole as whole.

Scoring issues: Score high for vision or values which draw links across the whole organisation; score low if vision is fragmented, addresses only some areas or issues (e.g. financial results only) or only some dimensions (e.g. no reference to emotions, commitment, etc.).

Typical intervention models and techniques:

- whole-of-organisation strategy development

People - quality of internal and external relationships

Themes: satisfaction, conflict resolution

People / Efficient *(Dialogue)*

Cue-phrase: "Relationships and trust are easily created, supported and maintained"

Summary: "Makes the best use of relationships and trust": look at customer relationship management, reputation management, complaints/conflict resolution at all levels.

Scoring issues: Score high for cultures that support openness and transparency in all processes, and direct acknowledgement and resolution of conflict; score low for 'fire-fighting', high level of complaints, cynicism about processes for promotion and other 'people issues', or for poor conflict-resolution.

Typical intervention models and techniques:

- privacy
- reputation-management
- 'Cluetrain' tactics
- leadership development

People / Reliable *(Leadership)*

Cue-phrase: "Relationships are grounded in balanced 'fair exchange'"

Summary: "Relationships and trust are consistent and reliable": look for balance and imbalance in transactions, especially for danger-signs such as one-sided 'agreements' or contracts that give short-term gain at the expense of long-term trust.

Scoring issues: Score high for 'win/win'; score low for 'win/lose' or 'lose/win', also for any tendency to treat relational assets as physical – "Our people are our greatest asset!"

Typical intervention models and techniques:

- integrity / ethics training
- shift to win/win perspective

People / Elegant *(Power/Property/Responsibility)*

Cue-phrase: "Personal element of relationships is supported"

Summary: "Relationships support the human element": look at work/life balance, conflict resolution, personalisation of work-space, personalisation of customer relationships, engagement in community issues.

Scoring issues: Score high for mutual emotional commitment and for personal focus; score low for impersonal 'business only', also for 'long hours' culture or a sense of 'emotional labour'.

Typical models and techniques:

- CRM systems
- customer-relationship training
- work/life balance
- personalisation

People / Appropriate *(Vision and values)*

Cue-phrase: "Relationships support business purpose"

Summary: "Relationships and trust support purpose and identity": look for processes to identify alignment with vision, values and purpose in hiring, firing, customer relationships, selection of in-vestors and business-partners, relationships with government and government officials; also danger-signs such as bribery and 'inducements' in relationships.

Scoring issues: Score high for values-based prioritisation of relat-ionships; score low for 'anything goes' opportunistic relationships, or for short-term 'inducements'.

Typical intervention models and techniques:

- customer-value analysis
- principle-based employment / stakeholder-relationships

People / Integrated *(Narrative)*

Cue-phrase: "Relationships and 'feel' help to bring every-thing together"

Summary: "Relationships and 'feel' are linked with purpose, prac-tice and knowledge": look for unifying symbols such as branding, slogans and catch-phrases used across the whole enterprise; also for signs of covert or dysfunctional power relationships.

Scoring issues: Score high for strong internal branding, especially for 'bottom-up' integration; score low for fragmented 'feel' or for 'emotion-free' workspaces.

Typical intervention models and techniques:

- customer-centric model
- 'wholeness responsibility'

Preparation - knowledge, planning, beliefs and mindset

Themes: knowledge audit, capability assessment, gap analysis

Preparation / Efficient *(Power/Property/Responsibility)*

Cue-phrase: "Support is provided for innovation, creativity and development of skills and knowledge"

Summary: "The best use is made of knowledge, planning, mindsets and beliefs": look at effective use and application of training and development, action research and action learning, knowledge management, process improvement.

Scoring issues: Score high for 'learning organisation', especially for support of 'bottom-up' innovation; score low for poor or non-existent knowledge management, inconsistent or inadequate training and development, or training for the sake of 'ticking the box'.

Typical intervention models and techniques:

- capability development, innovation training, systems thinking
- explicit 'development time'

Preparation / Reliable *(Active learning)*

Cue-phrase: "Knowledge provided is available, accurate and complete"

Summary: "Knowledge, planning, mindsets and beliefs help to deliver consistent, reliable results": look at intranets and similar knowledge-delivery systems, and support for both explicit and tacit knowledge; also look at audit and review processes to update and verify knowledge, to optimise workflows and to identify and rectify gaps within realistic timeframes, and for integration of knowledge into work-practices.

Scoring issues: Score high for strong use of knowledge management and review, such that people know where and who to go to for information, and to critique and review it; score low if support is provided only for explicit knowledge (databases) or only for tacit knowledge (people); also score low for any tendency to control conceptual assets in the same way as for physical property.

Typical intervention models and techniques:

- knowledge-management (KM)
- knowledge audit / review
- integrated performance-support systems (IPSS)

Preparation / Elegant *(Dialogue)*

Cue-phrase: "Personal knowledge is recognised, supported and shared"

Summary: "The human elements of knowledge, beliefs and mind-sets are supported": look at support for tacit knowledge, such as skills/experience databases, 'Yellow Pages' directories, narrative and storytelling, and the important 'water-cooler conversations'; also at usability and clarity of information.

Scoring issues: Score high for recognition of personal knowledge *as personal*; score low attempts to force all knowledge into the explicit domain, or to 'own' personal knowledge; also score low poor usability, or for both under-provision and over-provision of information – e.g. email glut.

Typical intervention models and techniques:

- tacit KM – communities of practice, 'Yellow Pages' skills / expertise directories, weblogs

Preparation / Appropriate *(Strategy)*

Cue-phrase: "Knowledge and beliefs support business purpose"

Summary: "Knowledge planning, mindsets and beliefs support vision, values, purpose and identity": look at knowledge management strategy, knowledge-support for strategy and decision-making, selection-criteria for information-gathering.

Scoring issues: Score high for clear guidelines to drive reporting, information-gathering and analysis; score low for information-gathering for its own sake.

Typical intervention models and techniques:

- knowledge audit
- gap analysis

Preparation / Integrated *(Tactics)*

Cue-phrase: "Knowledge supports the whole enterprise"

Summary: "Knowledge, planning, mindsets and beliefs link everything together": look at the usefulness, usability and scope of enterprise reporting and feedback, the balance of confidentiality and transparency; also look for support for diversity and difference of beliefs and worldviews, and at foresight processes and whole-of-organisation strategy.

Scoring issues: Score high for openness and knowledge-sharing culture, and for whole-of-enterprise strategy; score low for 'divide and rule' secrecy, for narrow focus on financials and other single-axis reporting, for lack of feedback, or for tendencies towards 'groupthink'.

Typical intervention models and techniques:

- intranet/extranet and other shared KM
- security policy / review

Process - actions, resources and environment

Themes: resources, skills-base, operating environment

Process / Efficient *(Active learning)*

Cue-phrase: "Work-processes are efficient and support enterprise performance"

Summary: "Actions make the best use of energies, resources and environment": look at efficiency and workflow optimisation; also at processes for gathering, collating and aggregating transaction data, customer details, statistics and other work-related records, and for converting it to usable knowledge.

Scoring issues: Score high for systematic assessment and review; score low for low efficiency / 'fire-fighting'.

Typical intervention models and techniques:

- active learning (e.g. After Action Review)
- kaizen continuous improvement
- supply-chain analysis

Process / Reliable *(Power/Property/Responsibility)*

Cue-phrase: "Skills, resources and environment support consistent results"

Summary: "Actions, resources and environment help to deliver expected results consistently and sustainably": look at equipment reliability, physical workflow and work-environment, supply chains and adaptability for changing conditions.

Scoring issues: Score high for adaptive workflow and work environment; score low for poor reliability, materials wastage or poor environmental management

Typical intervention models and techniques:

- workflow analysis
- capability analysis
- scenario development
- risk/opportunity analysis

Process / Elegant *(Leadership)*

Cue-phrase: "Skills and resources are of suitable quality for each task"

Summary: "Actions, resources and environment support the human elements": look at quality of work environment, occupational health and safety, ergonomics and evidence for job satisfaction, and at processes to support development of appropriate personal skills; also look at production quality and aesthetics.

Scoring issues: Score high for workspace that is co-created, and for workflows that adapt to the person rather than requiring the person to adapt to the task; score low if workspace design is imposed – 'one size fits all' – or if quality of any kind is assigned a low priority.

Typical intervention models and techniques:

- post-compliance TQM (e.g. quality circles)
- occupational health and safety (OH&S)
- ergonomics, personalisation, IPSS

Process / Appropriate *(Commitment)*

Cue-phrase: "Tasks, skills, facilities and resources support purpose"

Summary: "Resources, actions, environment and support are aligned to the overall purpose": look for clear distinctions between efficiency and effectiveness; also for support for individual as well as collective purpose, for promotion and cultural support of 'fuzzy' boundaries between roles, and for development and reinforcement of personal responsibility in achieving collective outcomes.

Scoring issues: Score high for focus on effectiveness in relation to purpose, on shared responsibility and on 'big picture' awareness; score low for rigid task-oriented job descriptions, lack of autonomy in executing work, or over-focus on efficiency for its own sake.

Typical intervention models and techniques:

- strategic review – SWOT, SCORE etc
- large-group interventions (e.g. Future Search)

Process / Integrated *(Feedback)*

Cue-phrase: "Work-processes provide a focus for the whole enterprise"

Summary: "Competencies, facilities and resources support purpose, relationships and overall effectiveness": look at leadership processes, at support for 'shop floor' innovation and whole-of-enterprise workflow optimisation, and for generalists who provide links across organisational 'silos'.

Scoring issues: Score high for self-directed work-teams and other cross-functional integration; score low for rigid boundaries and 'turf wars'.

Typical intervention models and techniques:

- ISO-9000:2000
- post-compliance TQM

Performance - bringing it all together

Themes: benchmarks, scorecards, dashboards

Performance / Efficient *(Tactics)*

Cue-phrase: "Beliefs and business models support overall integration"

Summary: "The organisation makes the best use of all its energies and resources": look at impact and implications of mindsets, beliefs and mental-models on overall integration; in particular, identify energies and intangible resources that may be ignored or under-acknowledged, such as reputation, morale, commitment and personal knowledge.

Scoring issues: Score high if performance indicators include human and other intangible elements; score low for narrow-focus models such as 'enterprise as money-machine'; also score low if models tend to create fragmentation or if support for generalists is poor.

Typical intervention models and techniques:

- benchmarking
- real-time 'dashboards'
- integration frameworks

Performance / Reliable *(Feedback)*

Cue-phrase: "Everyone is involved in system-wide feed-back and reflection"

Summary: "Bringing everything together delivers sustainable results": look for whole-of-organisation processes to leverage past experience for future growth and development.

Scoring issues: Score high for use of large-group interventions and systematic knowledge-sharing for process optimisation; score low for rigid top-down command-and-control management styles.

Typical intervention models and techniques:

- enterprise-wide 'dashboards'
- interactive intranet / extranet (e.g. wiki, chat, conferencing)
- narrative and dialogue
- large-group interventions (e.g. Open Space)

Performance / Elegant *(Narrative)*

Cue-phrase: "Integration supports diversity of skills, background and experience"

Summary: "Bringing it all together supports the human elements": look at balance between uniformity and diversity, organisational support for and use of diversity in strategy and decision-making, and mutual respect and inclusion of cultures and subcultures; also look at support for personal integration, such as meditation, study sabbaticals and work/life balance.

Scoring issues: Score high for explicit use and management of diversity, and active support for personal integration and work/life balance; score low for imposed uniformity, for 'work-only' culture or for breakdown into fragmented 'tribes'

Typical intervention models and techniques:

- equity/diversity policy / practice
- complexity-system techniques (e.g. Cynefin / Cognitive Edge)

Performance / Appropriate *(Foresight)*

Cue-phrase: "Metrics indicate when the organisation is effective and 'on purpose'"

Summary: "Bringing it all together supports the overall purpose": look for clear distinctions between 'efficient' and 'effective', and at processes for whole-of-organisation optimisation and for linking people and practice to purpose; also look for events and symbols of overall integration or for celebrations of organisational 'heroes' and actions which exemplify enterprise vision and values.

Scoring issues: Score high for performance metrics linked to purpose; score low for over-focus on local efficiency at the expense of overall effectiveness.

Typical intervention models and techniques:

- real-time 'dashboards'
- performance in relation to standard maturity-models
- values / performance review

Performance / Integrated *(Power/Property/Responsibility)*

Cue-phrase: "Appropriate metrics support overall integration"

Summary: "Performance indicators link everything together": look at reporting criteria and scope of performance indicators, particularly for intangibles; also at distinctions between lag- and lead-indicators, and usefulness and usability of metrics to guide pro-active strategy and the forward view.

Scoring issues: Score high for multi-axis reporting and emphasis on lead-indicators; score low for narrow focus on financials and other lag-indicators.

Typical intervention models and techniques:

- SEMPER
- Extended Balanced Scorecard
- Triple Bottom Line
- AA1000

SEMPER-5 ASSESSMENT

For details on use of this form, see 'SEMPER-5' in *SEMPER and SCORE: enhancing enterprise effectiveness* (Tetradian Books, 2008).

Organisation / enterprise:

Purpose / context:

Prepared by:

Date:

84

Purpose - vision, values, purpose and identity

Efficient - Vision, values and purpose are clear, simple and easy to apply in practice

Example description	Score	Trend
"Vision provides me with clear guidelines for day-to-day actions"	5	
"The enterprise values make sense to me"	4	
"I know what is expected of me at work"	3	
"There's not much connection between what we say and what we do"	2	
"This job pays my mortgage – that's it"	1	

Reliable - Vision, values and purpose provide clear guidelines to manage change

Example description	Score	Trend
"We embrace change but hold steadfast to our values"	5	
"Our values help us to manage change"	4	
"There's a cost-benefit analysis to everything we do"	3	
"We're always looking for the 'next best thing'"	2	
"We're rudderless, drifting from crisis to crisis"	1	

Elegant - Vision, values and purpose inspire personal commitment by members

Example description	Score	Trend
"I belong here - the reason I work here is to put these values into practice"	5	
"The values help me feel that I contribute, that what I do matters"	4	
"I know what our vision and values are"	3	
"We have a vision statement somewhere, don't we?"	2	
"It's every man for himself out here"	1	

Appropriate - Vision, values and purpose include social, environmental and global concerns

Example description	Score	Trend
"What we do here creates constructive change for the world"	5	
"We feel we're part of our community, and the community's part of us"	4	
"Our corporate philanthropy includes paid time for staff to do volunteer work"	3	
"What's good for the company is good for the community"	2	
"We're only here to make the shareholders rich"	1	

Integrated - Vision, values and purpose anchor all aspects of the enterprise

Example description	Score	Trend
"The strength of our culture is what makes everything happen"	5	
"Everyone knows what part they play in supporting each others' goals"	4	
"I know the part I play in supporting the organisation's goals"	3	
"Every decision means there'll be winners and losers - we balance that as best we can"	2	
"Every department has its own agenda - it's Us against Them"	1	

Notes / comments:

People - quality of internal and external relationships

Efficient - Relationships and trust are easily created, supported and maintained

Example description	Score	Trend
"Openness and trust are central to the way we work"	5	
"We can go straight to the top if there's any real problem"	4	
"We have good procedures to manage issues and complaints"	3	
"Sometimes you do have to watch what you say"	2	
"It's all about covering your ass round here"	1	

Reliable - Relationships are grounded in balanced 'fair exchange'

Example description	Score	Trend
"What goes round comes round - everything has to be fair to everyone"	5	
"People's time matters as much as money, so we dissuade the 'long hours' mindset"	4	
"We have a good benefits package for all staff, linked to our overall performance"	3	
"The pay seems fair enough, but there's no reward for effort"	2	
"Forget anyone else – their loss is our profit"	1	

Elegant - Personal element of relationships is supported

Example description	Score	Trend
"We get the best from everyone by working with all of who they are"	5	
"Emotions matter – we're encouraged to feel as well as think and do"	4	
"We're committed to improving work/life balance – people do have lives outside of work"	3	
"I'm recognised as being good at my job, but not really recognised as *me*"	2	
"I'm just a robot, a 'human resource'"	1	

Appropriate - Relationships support business purpose

Example description	Score	Trend
"Our relationships support our values, and vice versa"	5	
"We hire for attitude as much as for aptitude"	4	
"We have good systems for customer-relationship management and the like"	3	
"We'll do whatever it takes, as long as we don't actually sell our soul"	2	
"I don't care how you do it, just get it done"	1	

Integrated - Relationships and 'feel' help to bring everything together

Example description	Score	Trend
"Whoever we are, whatever we do, we're all representing the company at every moment"	5	
"We value our people as themselves, not as 'assets'"	4	
"Our people are our greatest asset!"	3	
"We get on well enough, but one group's needs tend to be met at another's expense"	2	
"Just constant bitching and backbiting – a real blame mentality"	1	

Notes / comments:

Preparation - knowledge, planning, beliefs and mindset

Efficient - Support is provided for innovation, creativity and development of skills and knowledge

Example description	Score	Trend
"Learning and innovation are a way of being, throughout the whole enterprise"	5	
"We actively learn from others and from our own mistakes"	4	
"We have opportunities to experiment and learn to do our work better"	3	
"You can sometimes try a new idea, but heaven help you if it doesn't work"	2	
"Check your brain in at the door"	1	

Reliable - Knowledge provided is available, accurate and complete

Example description	Score	Trend
"The knowledge system adapts itself to what I need, as I need it"	5	
"I can 'drill down' for further advice and information when I need it"	4	
"I have the information I need to do my work right"	3	
"I can never be certain it's current and complete"	2	
"I spend most of my time trying to find the right information"	1	

Elegant - Personal knowledge is recognised, supported and shared

Example description	Score	Trend
"Everyone is an expert in their own way, and we share that expertise in every way"	5	
"My knowledge, opinions and experience seem to count at work"	4	
"We have direct access to our experts"	3	
"I'm sure that someone has the information I need, I just don't know who"	2	
"The attitude is 'When I want your opinion I'll give it to you'"	1	

Appropriate - Knowledge and beliefs support business purpose

Example description	Score	Trend
"Our knowledge helps us to embrace change, to keep us 'on purpose'"	5	
"Our knowledge helps us to understand uncertainty"	4	
"Our knowledge helps us predict our future as best we can"	3	
"I guess someone must know why we collect all this data"	2	
"All I do is write reports that nobody reads"	1	

Integrated - Knowledge supports the whole enterprise

Example description	Score	Trend
"Open sharing of everyone's knowledge links the whole enterprise together"	5	
"I know how everyone contributes to the whole, the parts they play"	4	
"I know how I contribute to the whole, the part I play"	3	
"I can't see where my role fits into the bigger picture"	2	
"We're just mushrooms: kept in the dark with sh*t piled on top of us"	1	

Notes / comments:

Process - actions, resources and environment

Efficient - Work-processes are efficient and support enterprise performance

Example description	Score	Trend
"Everything we do is an opportunity to improve our work, our skills, ourselves"	5	
"New efficiencies sometimes come from the unexpected as well as from procedures"	4	
"We have a quality system that's accredited to ISO-9000 and other standards"	3	
"There must be a better way to do this..."	2	
"Just do it any way that gets the job out of the door"	1	

Reliable - Skills, resources and environment support consistent results

Example description	Score	Trend
"The system adapts itself to changing needs and conditions"	5	
"We can pull a system together quickly for almost anything"	4	
"We have the skills, materials and equipment we need to do the job right"	3	
"It's like 'You can have any colour you like as long as it's black'"	2	
"The system is so antiquated, it must have come out of the Ark"	1	

Elegant - Skills and resources are of suitable quality for each task

Example description	Score	Trend
"Quality isn't a job, it's a way of life, a way of being"	5	
"We know that quality is everyone's responsibility at work"	4	
"We're committed to doing quality work, and quality at work"	3	
"I take pride in my own work, anyway, even if no-one else does"	2	
"Close enough is good enough – they won't notice the difference"	1	

Appropriate - Tasks, skills, facilities and resources support purpose

Example description	Score	Trend
"Everyone feels personally responsible for whatever happens"	5	
"Everyone can pitch in together if it's needed"	4	
"Our guidelines allow us some leeway to give the customer better service"	3	
"We try to do the best we can within the rules"	2	
"If it's not in my job-description it's nothing to do with me"	1	

Integrated - Work-processes provide a focus for the whole enterprise

Example description	Score	Trend
"Practical issues provide us with a focus to develop the whole enterprise"	5	
"We also look to other industries for new ways to optimise our work"	4	
"We share best practice across our whole enterprise"	3	
"Improvements in one place just seem to make things worse elsewhere"	2	
"Why should we be interested in anyone else's problems?"	1	

Notes / comments:

Performance - bringing it all together

Efficient - Beliefs and business models support overall integration

Example description	Score	Trend
"Benchmarks can be useful, but they focus on the past, not the future"	5	
"We benchmark our performance against world's best practice in any industry"	4	
"We benchmark our performance against our industry competitors"	3	
"We benchmark our performance against the previous quarter"	2	
"Benchmarks? – we don't have time to waste on that stuff"	1	

Reliable - Everyone is involved in system-wide feedback and reflection

Example description	Score	Trend
"We involve everyone in improving overall performance"	5	
"We move whole teams around to gain different perspectives"	4	
"Our managers are encouraged to walk round to gain different perspectives"	3	
"We do performance surveys, but nothing much seems to come from them"	2	
"It's a 'Shut up and do what you're told' mentality"	1	

Elegant - Integration supports diversity of skills, background and experience

Example description	Score	Trend
"What's diversity? (Isn't it people just being who they are?)"	5	
"We use our staff's diversity and background to support our business goals"	4	
"We have compliance with best practice on equity and diversity"	3	
"Each department tends to form its own clique, its own clan"	2	
"What's diversity?"	1	

Appropriate - Metrics indicate when the enterprise is effective and 'on purpose'

Example description	Score	Trend
"Our successes and failures help to remind us of who we are and what we stand for"	5	
"We're doing okay as long as we remember to celebrate our successes"	4	
"We're doing okay as long as we keep to strategy and ahead of change"	3	
"We're doing okay as long as we meet our department's quarterly targets"	2	
"All we do is chase our tails"	1	

Integrated - Appropriate metrics support overall integration

Example description	Score	Trend
"Measuring intangibles tells us the health of our culture and our place in the world"	5	
"Measuring tangibles and intangibles together helps us make sense of where we are"	4	
"We do regular audits of intangibles like reputation, satisfaction and brand awareness"	3	
"We sometimes do staff satisfaction surveys, but I don't know if anyone reads them"	2	
"Measuring touchy-feely stuff is a waste of time – shareholder value is all that matters"	1	

Notes / comments:

SEMPER-11

Overview

SEMPER-11 – also known as Standard SEMPER – provides a more detailed view of the enterprise innerstructure and its present and likely future condition, its overall 'ability to do work'.

> Note, though, that unlike the simple pick-from-a-list scoring in SEMPER-5, scoring in SEMPER-11 relies on a detailed personal assessment of the entire context by the consultant, and is likely to have a much broader impact on the enterprise.
>
> In practice, the assessment needs to draw on experience from a very broad range of domains, including complexity-science, general-systems theory, organisational psychology, narrative knowledge and many other specialist sources. So although I've included SEMPER-11 in this book for completeness, and to give a taste of what is possible with the full SEMPER framework, I need to warn you that it really should be used only by accredited practitioners.
>
> You're welcome to experiment with SEMPER-11 as-is, as described here, but only on the proviso that the results are out of our control, and cannot be guaranteed. Fair enough?

The end-result of the diagnostic is a 'dashboard' of the current state of the enterprise.

By mapping tools and techniques to SEMPER-11 domains, the diagnostic also provides a means to target interventions with more precision than is usually available with conventional approaches.

Structure

A SEMPER-11 assessment covers eleven distinct domains, as defined by the tetradian framework:

- the four *dimensions*: behavioural/physical, conceptual/mental, relational/emotional, and aspirational/spiritual;
- the six *link-themes* between those dimensions: vision and values, leadership, active learning, narrative and dialogue, sensemaking and foresight, responsibility and empowerment; and

- an overview-domain of *integration* between all the dimensions and link-themes.

The assessment asks the same five questions about the effectiveness of activities in the domain:

- Is it efficient?
- Is it reliable?
- Is it elegant?
- Is it appropriate?
- Is it integrated well with other domains?

In the SEMPER-11 diagnostic, these questions are presented as cue-phrases, matched to the respective issues in the domain. Each domain can be assessed separately, with the assessment supported by other exploratory questions about the domain, and generic 'relevance' questions which apply to all domains.

Assessment and interventions

The following notes summarise assessment criteria for each SEMPER-11 domain, and questions to review the relevance of each context to the whole. Each section also describes typical business issues that are associated with the respective domain, examples of models and techniques commonly used to address issues in that domain, and the kinds of benefits that would result from doing so.

To conduct the assessment, select a starting domain, dependent on the identified issue or 'problem'. Then:

1. explore the selected domain, using the questions indicated by the domain

2. use the generic relevance questions derived from the R⁵ keywords (recursion, rotation, reflexion, reciprocation, resonance) to explore in greater depth
   [note: because these questions are generic to all domains, they are on a separate linked page at the end of the summaries]

3. use that domain's variant of the LEARN keywords (efficient, reliable, elegant, appropriate, integrated) to evaluate the context, using a 1-5 scale for each; mark the score appropriately on the diagnostic
   [on the paper form, circle the respective score; on the online version, select the score from the dropdown list]

4. optionally, assign a trend-adjustment for each score: +1 for improving, 0 for stable, or -1 for worsening
   [on the paper form, write the respective trend-adjustment; on the online version, select the trend-value from the dropdown list]
5. move to a related tetradian domain (i.e. to one of the three link-themes if a dimension, to one of the two linked dimensions if a link-theme, or to overall integration etc)

Repeat this sequence until all domains and the overall integration have been assessed.

See *SEMPER-11 assessment* (p.115) for a set of example forms that can be used for SEMPER-11 assessments.

Aspirational dimension – identity and purpose

The core business issue here is that identity and purpose are essential to define 'effective' within the context.

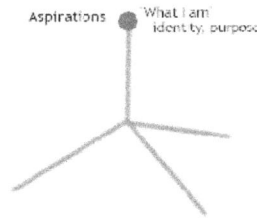

Aspirational or spiritual assets include anything which supports the definition of identity and purpose, and the relationship of Self to Self (whatever Self may be in the context). In tangible form, this includes corporate identity; logos and branding; vision, mission and values statements (see *Vision and Values*); strategy documents (see *Sensemaking and foresight*) and policies on acceptable and unacceptable behaviours (see *Responsibility and empowerment*). Intangible assets include morale, commitment and overall 'health and fitness' of the enterprise.

Questions

- *Who is 'We', or 'Us'?* – For an individual, use "Who is 'I'?", and change 'We' or 'Us' to 'I' in subsequent questions.
- *How is 'We' defined? What are the boundaries between 'Us' and 'not-Us'?* – Look also for boundaries between members / 'insiders' and non-members / 'outsiders'.
- *How are these boundaries between 'Us' and 'not-Us' maintained? How is the integrity of 'Us' maintained?* – This includes both internal integrity (morale, health etc) and external (self-protection, etc).
- *What do 'We' stand for? What is the purpose for 'Us' in existing?* – In a commercial context, emphasise the need to move beyond "making money" as a purpose; financial performance is not a

viable purpose in itself, but an outcome of a wider overall purpose.

- *How are aspirational assets such as morale measured and maintained?* – Note any mistaken tendency to treat aspirational/spiritual properties as physical – for example, acting as if morale can be bought, sold or transferred to others.

Business focus

- Organisational restructure
- Mergers and acquisitions
- Value webs
- Brand development
- Creating a new team or business unit
- Joining or leaving a team or organisation
- Start and end of a project
- Aspirational assets – morale, organisational health, etc

Typical models and techniques

- Visioning processes
- Spiritual Intelligence (Zohar et al.)
- Brainstorming and related techniques
- Personal development processes
- Role/Mask workshops

Benefits generated

- Clarity and focus on purpose
- Greater effectiveness

Relational dimension – internal and external relationships

Relations

"How I relate" - relationships

The key business issue here is that performance and profitability are tightly correlated with quality of relationships, whether internal (staff, employees), intermediate (business partners, consultants, share-holders) or external (customers, suppliers, other stakeholders).

Relational or emotional assets include anything which defines and supports relationships between Self and Other. (In a collective, the 'Other' may be internal, intermediate or external, as above.) In a

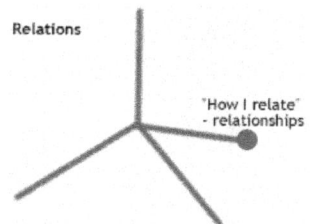

tangible form, these may represented by images such as brands; by documents such as contracts, or exchanges of telephone calls and emails; customer and employment records; or simply by physical presence. However, the assets themselves are invariably intangible, as they indicate trust *between* entities rather than as an attribute of some specific entity. Relational assets may also be either two-way and mutual, or one-way from or towards the Self (as in reputation or commitment to a brand). All relational assets are volatile over time, and will usually need regular maintenance.

Questions

- *What relationships with others are needed in order to support the purpose?* – Include and distinguish between internal, intermediate and external relationships.
- *What form do these relationships take?* – Identify content (e.g. documents, records, web-server logs) that indicates existence and status of each asset.
- *In what ways are relationships structured?* – Include formal structures (e.g. hierarchies, contracts) and informal networks (e.g. communities of practice).
- *How are relational assets measured and maintained?* – Include one-way relationships towards Self but outside the control of the Self, such as reputation; note also any tendency to treat relational/emotional properties as physical – for example, where "Our people are our greatest asset!" is mistaken for an asset to buy from or sell to others.
- *In what ways are shared successes acknowledged and celebrated?* – Identify especially celebrations of 'heroes' who exemplify the organisation's values and purpose

Business focus

- Workplace relations
- Business partnerships
- Market renewal
- Customer relationships
- Community relations
- Relational assets – relationships, reputation, trust etc

Typical models and techniques

- Emotional Intelligence (Goleman et al.)
- 360° feedback
- Industrial psychology

- Social network analysis/social network applications
- Communities of practice
- Weblogs
- Community forums

Benefits generated

- Clarity on roles and responsibilities
- Self-propagating marketing and public relations
- Improved reputation management

Conceptual dimension – knowledge and mindset

Knowledge is a key differentiator for competitive advantage. Beliefs and worldviews also underpin what is perceived as possible and not-possible.

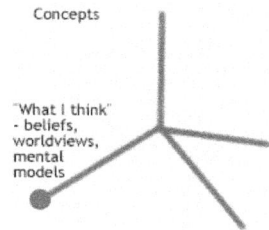

Conceptual assets include anything which expresses some form of knowledge, or supports knowledge, belief and other relationships between Self and idea. In tangible form (explicit knowledge), this includes patents, trademarks and other intellectual property; libraries, databases and documents; and also financial records and other forms of organisational history. As history, knowledge tends to represent the past, but may need to focus on the future (see *Sense-making and foresight*) or the immediate present (see *Active learning*). Most conceptual assets are intangible (tacit knowledge), usually reside only within or between people (see *Narrative and dialogue*) and may well be inexpressible in explicit form.

Questions

- *What records, information, knowledge and beliefs are needed to support the purpose?* – Include and distinguish between each type of asset, and between explicit and tacit forms of these; also include assets needed for creativity and innovation, for organisational history and for external compliance.
- *To what extent are these assets available for the organisation? How are these assets identified, created, maintained, distributed and shared?* – Include support both for explicit assets – e.g. databases, 'best practice' – and tacit assets (see next question).
- *What support is provided for the social processes of knowledge?* – Include social-networks, communities-of-practice and other human-centred forms of knowledge management.

- *What processes exist to determine what knowledge to share, and with whom?* – Cross-links to organisational purpose are crucial here, especially in complex value-web relationships.
- *To what extent does the business-model depend on withholding access to knowledge?* – Business-models that depend on withholding of conceptual assets – for security reasons, to increase sale-value, etc – are inherently fragile because of the tendency of all knowledge to migrate to the public domain.

Business focus

- Organisational knowledge
- Creativity and innovation
- Document management
- Organisational performance – scorecards, statistics etc
- Conceptual assets – Intellectual property (trademarks, patents, processes etc), innovation capabilities

Typical models and techniques

- Multi-axis reporting – Balanced Scorecard, Global Reporting Initiative, etc
- Knowledge inventories and audits
- Business intelligence, competitive intelligence
- Scenario/strategic planning
- Brainstorming and related techniques
- Intranet/extranet design and development
- Indexing and taxonomies

Benefits generated

- Improved knowledge availability
- Improved adaptability, resilience
- Support for strategy development

Behavioural dimension – actions, resources and environment

The key business issue here is efficiency and optimisation of business practice.

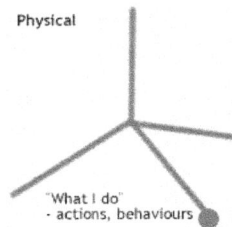

Physical

"What I do" - actions, behaviours

Behavioural and physical assets include anything which supports execution and tangible business activity, such as physical resources, facilities and equipment; environment and workspace; competencies and skill-sets; processes, workflows and transactions; and physical energy

101

and infrastructure needed to support the tasks – electricity, gas, transport, data-cabling, etc. This would also include financial resources, as part of the means to obtain those more tangible resources.

Most of these assets are directly tangible, and all are measurable in quantitative terms. However, precisely because they *are* tangible and measurable, there is often an over-emphasis on these assets, to the detriment of overall integration. This may also be seen as an over-emphasis on local efficiency or cost-control at the expense of overall effectiveness.

Questions

- *What resources, skill-sets and other physical assets are needed to support the purpose?* – Include and distinguish between each type of asset, and the tasks for which each is required.
- *How are these assets identified, obtained, maintained, distributed and shared?* – Note especially the assets and transactions in multi-party supply-chains and value-webs
- *To what extent are these assets available to the organisation as needed?* – Assess redundancy and backup, storage needs, just-in-time resource management etc for workflows
- *What physical facilities and environment are needed to support each task?* – Include and assess issues such as health and safety, workflow traffic, personal / shared space, morale etc
- *How are these environmental resources identified, obtained, maintained, and shared?* – Note especially the extent to which individuals are involved in creating their own workspace and workflow
- *What processes are used to optimise transactions, workflows and environment?* – Effectiveness depends on continuous reassessment of efficiency, especially in fast-changing contexts'

Business focus

- Workflow efficiency
- Post-merger process integration
- Workplace environment
- Physical assets – equipment, materials, resources, finances

Typical models and techniques

- Process mapping, process re-engineering
- Workflow analysis

- Workspace design

Benefits generated

- Improved efficiency
- Reduced error-rates
- Clarity on roles and responsibilities

Vision and values

An enterprise is essentially a collection of relationships brought together for a common purpose. Vision and values provide the bonds that hold these relationships together, and underpin both the enterprise's internal culture and its relations with its intermediate and external stakeholders.

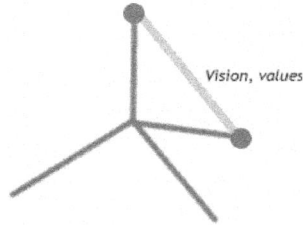

Vision, values

Distinctions need to be drawn between vision, purpose, missions and goals. Vision must be 'larger' than the enterprise, as it provides an anchor for relationships with stakeholders; purpose is how the enterprise sees itself in relation to that 'world picture' (see *Aspirations – identity and purpose*), whilst missions and goals define short-term strategies and tactics (see *Sense-making and foresight*).

Questions

- *How do aspirations support relationships, and vice versa?* – Vision and values should provide a bridge for mutual support and optimisation of these assets
- *In what ways are vision and values defined?* – Note any formal statements of vision and values, but also assess implicit values in the culture
- *What distinctions are drawn between vision, purpose, mission, goal?* – Failure to distinguish appropriately between these is a common cause of ineffectiveness
- *What differences exist between what the organisation says, and what it does?* – Assess differences between espoused and actual values, vision, etc
- *What processes are used to review and revise vision and values?* – Assess also who is and is not included in such processes
- *In what contexts are overall vision and values reassessed and revised?* – Common examples include merger/acquisition, regular whole-of-organisation meetings, etc

- *In what ways do vision and values support commitment and 'ownership'?* – Assess the impact of vision and values on everyday decision-making and work-practice
- *In what ways do vision and values reflect work/life balance and other 'external' themes?* – Assess the extent to which the 'whole person' and the wider community are acknowledged at work

Business focus

- Adaptability and resilience in fast-changing markets
- Business ethics
- Motivation and alignment
- Work/life balance
- Partnerships with community, suppliers and other stakeholders
- Post-merger integration
- Outsourcing

Typical models and techniques

- Visioning processes
- Large-group intervention (Open Space, Future Search, etc.)
- Values/ethics audit
- Complex-facilitation and related emergent techniques (Cynefin Discovery, etc.)

Benefits generated

- Improved motivation and alignment
- Reduced absenteeism
- Greater versatility and adaptability
- Simpler, clearer contractual relationships
- Reduced risk
- Increased stakeholder tolerance for errors

Skills and leadership

Leadership may take a variety of different forms: for example, coaching and mentoring, to assist others to develop their skills (see *Active learning*) and responsibilities (see *Empowerment and responsibility*); 'holding the vision' for a group or team (see *Vision and values*); innovation and development of

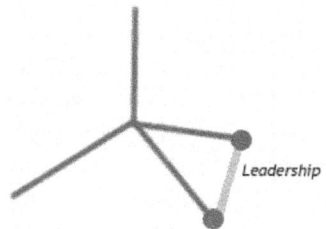

strategy and tactics (see *Sense-making and foresight*); or creating inspirational stories (see *Narrative and dialogue*).

However, in this context, leadership is primarily the means through which relationships are expressed in action, leading Self and others through successive stages of a workflow or overall task. One variant of this is the usual managerial role, with its emphasis on the immediate issues of productivity and process, but different styles of leadership are needed in each stage of the classic Group Dynamics cycle of Forming, Storming, Norming, Performing and Adjourning.

Questions

- *How do relationships support actions, environment and resources, and vice versa?* – Leadership should provide a bridge for mutual support and optimisation of these assets
- *In what ways do structured relationships support leadership?* – Assess and compare formal structures (e.g. hierarchy) and informal structures (e.g. communities of practice)
- *In what ways is everyone a leader, and everyone recognised as a leader?* – Also assess who is identified as 'leaders', by whom, whether formally or informally, and in what contexts
- *In what ways do leadership roles and styles vary according to context?* – Assess context-dependent changes both of role and of structure (e.g. hierarchy vs self-organising team)
- *What impact do leadership styles have upon productivity and performance?* – Also assess measurements – if any – used for evaluation and review
- *What processes exist to develop leadership?* – Compare formal (e.g. training) and informal (e.g. coaching, mentoring) leadership development; also assess tools and techniques used to support this (e.g. psychological profiling, 360° feedback)

Business focus

- Empowerment
- Self-organising teams
- Organisational structure
- Leadership

Typical models and techniques

- Coaching and mentoring
- Leadership-style profiling (Belbin, Insights, etc)
- Situational leadership

- Principle-centred leadership (Covey et al.)
- Five Elements (Tetradian)

Benefits generated

- Improved effectiveness, responsiveness
- Improved morale

Active learning

Learning through reflection and feedback is the primary means through which efficiencies are created, product, skill and service quality improved, and safety enhanced.

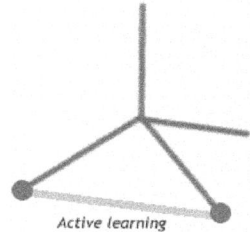

Active learning

Some form of self-reflection, either on an individual or a group level – such as in TQM, quality circles and after-action reviews – is usually the most effective approach, although this tends to be a domain of incremental improvement rather than quantum transformation. For the latter, some form of external analysis will usually be needed, as in business process re-engineering and classic 'scientific management' – though care needs to be taken to ensure that new processes are co-created (see *Leadership*) rather than imposed through 'edicts from above', in case inadvertent damage to *Responsibility and empowerment* counters any potential gains in productivity.

Questions

- *How does knowledge support actions, environment and resources, and vice versa?* – Active learning should provide a bridge for mutual support and optimisation of these assets
- *What processes exist to support team learning?* – Assess support for improvement as a collective rather than solely as individuals (e.g. system improvement)
- *What processes exist to provide feedback for individual or collective improvement?* – Assess availability and quality of feedback from supervisors, co-workers, and the overall work-context
- *In what ways is improvement externally defined? In what ways is it co-created?* – Assess roles and relationships of external 'others' such as facilitators and analysts in process improvement; assess also the extent to which local knowledge and experience is used and applied in innovation
- *In what ways is learning grounded in practice?* – Identify support for 'thinking with the hands' as well as 'thinking with head'

- *What facilities and processes exist to support skills development in 'safe space'?* – Assess options such as simulation, role-play and 'sandbox' practice-grounds
- *What is the balance between intermittent and continuous skills development?* – Compare event-based processes such as workshops or lectures with continuous learning-in-action
- *What theoretical models are used to assess options for improvement?* – Examples include workflow mapping, time and motion study, action research and after-action review

Business focus

- Skills development
- Product or service quality
- Workflow innovation
- *Kaizen* continuous improvement
- Occupational health and safety

Typical models and techniques

- Action-learning/action-research
- TQM (Deming et al.)
- Quality-circles
- Role-play
- Simulation

Benefits generated

- Improved knowledge creation, capture and retention
- Stronger teamwork
- Improved capabilities
- Improved engagement
- Faster acquisition of skills

Narrative and dialogue

Personal stories provide not only a history of transactions and relationships, but also a core source of organisational knowledge. It's also true that "markets are conversations" – and those relationships in turn, especially in the longer term, depend on the openness and honesty of the co-created stories.

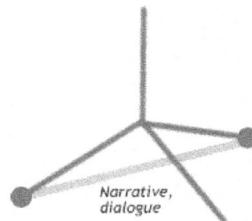

Narrative, dialogue

Stories are often layered, creating knowledge linking best-practice or worst-practice with the culture's deep myths and beliefs. By definition, tacit knowledge is personal – "people know more than they can say, and can say more than they can write down" – and often created with others in an emergent process developing over time; hence interpersonal relations and people-management issues are often also crucial to an organisation's management of its collective knowledge.

Questions

- *How do relationships support knowledge, and vice versa?* – Narrative and dialogue should provide a bridge for mutual support and optimisation of these assets
- *What facilities exist to manage, maintain and share tacit knowledge?* – Examples include communities of practice, weblogs, social network applications, expertise directories
- *What processes exist to create and elicit shared knowledge?* – Examples include Bohm dialogue, large-group intervention (e.g. Open Space), narrative enquiry
- *In what ways are 'outsiders' engaged in the organisation's stories and history?* – Assess themes such as marketing, stakeholder engagement, public relations and reputation management
- *How are the boundaries between 'inside' and 'outside' managed in creating knowledge?* – Assess themes such as partnering, value webs, co-design, demand innovation and viral marketing
- *What processes exist to identify and manage 'anti-stories'?* – Assess the impact and validity of alternate views and sub-cultures, counter-myths and 'shadow networks'
- *What processes exist to ensure openness and transparency in all relationships?* – Assess tendencies to secrecy, and nominal 'winners' and 'losers' from such secrecy

Business focus

- Product/service innovation
- Stakeholder engagement
- Reputation management

Typical models and techniques

- Communities of practice (Wenger, Sengé et al)
- Cynefin narrative enquiry (Snowden/IBM)
- Dialogue process (Bohm et al.)
- Demand innovation (Slywotzky et al.)

- Viral marketing (Godin, Locke et al.)
- Weblogs

Benefits generated

- Improved public relations
- Proactive innovation
- Stronger internal/external alignment

Sense-making and foresight

The key concern here is to create a balance between the aspirations for the future and the knowledge of the past. The end-result of these processes is strategy and tactics.

Unlike *Vision and values*, which are anchored in feelings, strategy is anchored in knowledge. Selection of tools and techniques depends greatly on the context. Traditional 'top-down' strategic planning still works well in stable, low-change environments; but most enterprises will need the greater versatility and adaptability of emergent techniques derived from complexity science, which in turn depend on a broader diversity of views and experience to create bridges between over-specialised 'silos'.

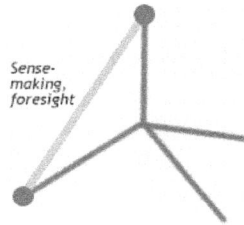

Questions

- *How do identity and purpose support knowledge, and vice versa?* – Sense-making and foresight should provide a bridge for mutual support and optimisation of these assets
- *Who is involved in development of strategy?* – Assess the scope of engagement (e.g. top management only, managers, other staff, suppliers, etc.)
- *What processes are used to gather and collate knowledge for strategy?* – Examples include business intelligence, focus groups, large-group interventions (e.g. Future Search)
- *In what ways does the strategy acknowledge and allow for emergence and uncertainty?* – Assess the resilience of strategy, the extent to which it can self-adapt proactively to changing contexts
- *What processes are used to make sense of inherent uncertainty?* – Examples include scenario development, Cynefin sense-making, causal layered analysis, Bohm dialogue

- *What processes are used to identify needed skills, resources, relationships, knowledge?* – Assess especially the roles of generalists in bridging specialist 'silos'
- *What processes are used to partition strategy into detailed actions?* – Assess the breakdown of strategy into vision, purpose, missions and goals for each actor in the strategy
- *What processes are used to ensure alignment with and commitment to the strategy?* – Assess and compare 'top-down' command-and-control with consensus and engagement
- *In what ways do the culture's beliefs, deep myths and stories affect strategy?* – Assess also the impact on strategy implementation of differences between espoused and actual values

Business focus

- Complex/intractable issues – culture etc.
- Strategic direction
- Organisational effectiveness

Typical models and techniques

- Scenario development (Schwartz et al.)
- Strategic conversation (Hamel, Prahalad, van der Heijden et al.)
- Cynefin sense-making (Snowden/IBM)
- Causal Layered Analysis (Inayatullah et al.)
- Large group interventions (World Café, Open Space etc.)

Benefits generated

- Clarity of direction
- Improved alignment, consensus and commitment
- Proactive response and resilience

Responsibility and empowerment

Responsibility, empowerment

The key issue here is personal power – 'the ability to do work' in appropriate ways, with choice, responsibility and purpose.

Empowerment and responsibility are supported and developed through *Active learning* and *Leadership*, but their roots are in purpose and practice. Ultimately, 'the ability to do work' arises only from within the Self, but support is usually needed to bring it out. Power-transactions between individuals

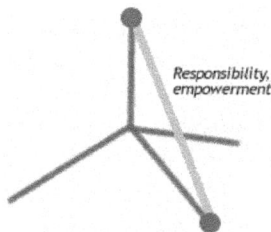

are always either power-with (mutual support or 'win/win') or power-against (mutual destruction or 'lose/lose'). Productivity depends on support for power-with; power-against becomes prevalent, in forms such as bullying, back-biting and 'office politics', whenever the link to shared purpose is lost and power is seen only as 'external' to Self (the 'win/lose' delusion).

Questions

- *How do actions, resources, environment support identity and purpose, and vice versa?* – Responsibility, empowerment should provide a bridge for mutual support and optimisation of these assets
- *What beliefs are held about the source of personal power and collective power?* – Contrast views of source as external (power is 'given' or 'taken') or internal (personal responsibility)
- *To what extent is the workspace managed through mutual respect?* – Other useful keywords to identify 'power-with' include empowerment, compassion, love and humility
- *To what extent is the workspace managed through fear?* – Other useful keywords to identify 'power-against' include domination, manipulation and blame
- *To what extent is self-denigration or self-doubt an issue here?* – Identify any tendency towards 'lose/win' as well as 'win/lose'
- *What practices exist to support development of personal power and responsibility?* – Examples include meditation, martial arts, sports training, coaching and mentoring
- *What practices exist to support development of collective power and responsibility?* – Examples include large-group interventions such as Open Space, World Café and group dialogue
- *What processes exist to link practice to purpose?* – Purpose also provides links to vision and values, and to foresight and strategy

Business focus

- Personal productivity and commitment
- Interpersonal issues
- Office politics

Typical models and techniques

- Coaching and mentoring

- Personal disciplines and practices (meditation, martial arts, etc.)
- Power/response-ability (Tetradian)
- Seven Habits (Covey et al.)

Benefits generated

- Improved productivity
- Improved responsibility
- Minimisation of game-plays, bullying etc.

Integration - bringing it all together

'Think global, act local' applies as much to business integration as to anything else: whenever we plan and execute any intervention in any part of the organisation, we need to be aware of its effects on the whole.

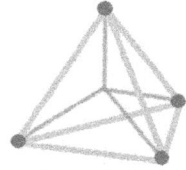

Two key requirements for integration are an appropriate framework, usually based on principles from complexity-science; and strong support for the generalists who create bridges between departments and specialities, and between ideas, skills, resources, relationships and alternate views of purpose. Overall effectiveness can rarely be achieved without these, as they provide the anchors for 'efficiency on purpose'.

Questions

- *What models and frameworks are used to create and maintain integration?* – Examples include Beer viable-systems model, Tetradian SEMPER, Sengé five disciplines
- *What whole-of-system support exists for integration?* – Assess mechanisms, if any, which support feedback and reflection between all parts of the organisation
- *In what ways does the organisation identify and support its generalists?* – Assess especially the absence of such support, such as performance against inappropriate metrics
- *What is the balance between formal and informal structures in the organisation?* – Formal structures provides anchors for organisation, but most work is done through informal structures
- *How is overall effectiveness monitored and managed?* – Assess usage, if any, of multi-axis metrics such as Balanced Scorecard

Business focus

- Organisational system and structure
- Overall effectiveness

Typical models and techniques

- Complexity science (emergence, biomimicry, non-linear systems etc.)
- Living organisation (Handy, de Geus et al.)
- Viable Systems model (Beer et al.)
- SEMPER model (Tetradian)

Benefits generated

- Provides consistent framework for interventions
- Improves effectiveness of overall organization

Assessing relevance

The R^5 keywords – recursion, rotation, reflexion, reciprocation, resonance – provide a focus through which to assess the relevance of the selected issue in relation to the whole. The five principles are derived from systems theory and complexity science, to extend and enhance the classic models of 'scientific management'. The following assessment questions combine various aspects of these principles.

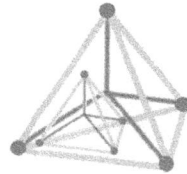

Questions

- *What is this an example of?* – Assess ways in which the same issues repeat on a larger scale
- *What is an example of this?* – Assess ways in which the same issues repeat on a smaller scale
- *How could this be simplified by learning from other examples of this?* – Assess options to create consistency or remove special cases through 'self-similarity' with related issues
- *What is another perspective on this?* – Rotate to a different view (e.g. from another department, customer, supplier, another culture or time)
- *What is not being acknowledged and addressed in this?* – Assess the 'undiscussables', especially issues and events projected or reflected onto others

- *What aspects of the whole can be seen in this?* – Assess ways in which themes of the whole organisation are reflected and exemplified in this issue
- *What is being exchanged, created, destroyed or transformed in this?* – Assess overall changes to types of assets or resources (e.g. morale created, relationships destroyed); also assess what types and quantities of assets and resources are exchanged, and by what or whom
- *Are all physical exchanges and transformations balanced in this?* – Assess system 'leakages' such as inefficiency, waste, pollution etc [Note: balance or imbalance may only occur over a whole system, or over time]
- *How is physical balance maintained and assured in this?* – Assess measures to identify, monitor and address any imbalance
- *Who 'wins' from transactions in this? How, and in what ways?* – Assess balance and reciprocity in non-physical and other non-zero-sum transactions (e.g. money, prestige)
- *How is 'win-win' created and assured within transactions in this?* – In non- zero-sum transactions, compare tendencies towards 'win-win' versus 'win-lose' (illusory 'lose-lose')
- *What are the responsibilities in this?* – Assess who is responsible for what, and how those responsibilities are identified, monitored and assured
- *How are the responsibilities balanced in this?* – Assess mutuality of responsibilities, especially any arbitrary assignment of 'rights' (i.e. non-responsibilities)

SEMPER-11 ASSESSMENT

For details on use of this form, see 'SEMPER-11' in *SEMPER and SCORE: enhancing enterprise effectiveness* (Tetradian Books, 2008)

Organisation / enterprise:

Purpose / context:

Prepared by:

Date:

Aspirations - identity and purpose

Dimension	Score	Trend
Efficient - Effort needed to maintain identity and purpose *Score high for easily / consistently maintained; low for high effort / 'fire-fighting'*	1 2 3 4 5	
Reliable - Identity and purpose consistently described and maintained *Score low for any tendency to treat aspirational assets as physical*	1 2 3 4 5	
Elegant - Identity and purpose understood / committed to by Self, others	1 2 3 4 5	
Appropriate – Identity and purpose linked to wider context *Score high for wider-scope awareness; low for Self / physical-only orientation*	1 2 3 4 5	
Integrated – Identity and purpose linked with all other aspects of the enterprise	1 2 3 4 5	

Notes / comments:

Relations - internal and external relationships

Dimension	Score	Trend
Efficient - Effort needed to create and maintain relationships and trust *Score high for easily / consistently maintained; low for high effort / 'fire-fighting'*	1 2 3 4 5	
Reliable - Relationships provide balanced 'fair exchange' *Score high for win/win; low for win/lose or lose/win; also score low for any tendency to treat relational assets as physical*	1 2 3 4 5	
Elegant - Personal element of relationships is supported *Score high for mutual emotional commitment; low for impersonal 'business only'*	1 2 3 4 5	
Appropriate - Relationships support business purpose	1 2 3 4 5	
Integrated – Relationships linked with all other aspects of the enterprise	1 2 3 4 5	

Notes / comments:

Concepts - knowledge and mindset

Dimension	Score	Trend
Efficient - Effort needed to create / maintain knowledge and innovation *Score high for easily / consistently maintained; low for high effort / 'fire-fighting'*	1 2 3 4 5	
Reliable - Knowledge provided is available, accurate and complete *Score low if support is provided only for explicit knowledge or only for tacit knowledge; also score low for any tendency to treat conceptual assets as physical*	1 2 3 4 5	
Elegant - Knowledge provided is usable, relevant and in sufficient detail *Score low for both under-provision and over-provision of information - e.g. email glut*	1 2 3 4 5	
Appropriate - Knowledge and beliefs support business purpose *Also score low if multi-axis reporting - e.g. Balanced Scorecard - is not used*	1 2 3 4 5	
Integrated – Shared knowledge linked with all other aspects of the enterprise	1 2 3 4 5	

Notes / comments:

Behaviours - actions and environment

Dimension	Score	Trend
Efficient - Effort needed to create and maintain skills, physical assets *Score high for easily / consistently maintained; low for high effort / 'fire-fighting'*	1 2 3 4 5	
Reliable - Skills, resources and environment are consistently available	1 2 3 4 5	
Elegant - Skills and resources are of suitable quality for each task *Also score high if workspace design is co-created; low if design is imposed*	1 2 3 4 5	
Appropriate - Competencies, facilities and resources support purpose *Score high for 'big picture' awareness; low for over-focus on efficiency for its own sake*	1 2 3 4 5	
Integrated – Facilities, skills and resources linked with all other aspects of the enterprise	1 2 3 4 5	

Notes / comments:

Vision and values

Dimension	Score	Trend
Efficient - Clear distinctions between vision, purpose, mission, goal *Score low where missions or goals are presented as vision or business-purpose*	1 2 3 4 5	
Reliable - Espoused and actual vision and values are consistent *Score low for high divergence between espoused and actual vision or values*	1 2 3 4 5	
Elegant - All stakeholders engaged in creating vision and values *Score high for regular whole-of-organisation engagement; low for top-down imposition; also score low if not connecting to needs and concerns of external stakeholders*	1 2 3 4 5	
Appropriate - Vision and values provide guidelines to manage change *Also score low if vision and values are abstract and disconnected from actual practice*	1 2 3 4 5	
Integrated – Vision and values linked with all other aspects of the enterprise	1 2 3 4 5	

Notes / comments:

Skills and leadership

Dimension	Score	Trend
Efficient - Feedback is provided to develop leadership	1 2 3 4 5	
Reliable - Leadership changes according to the context *Score high for context-dependent leader, low for single-leader model (e.g. hierarchical)*	1 2 3 4 5	
Elegant - Everyone leads in their own way *Also score high for contextual/situational choice of leadership style; low for fixed model (e.g. hierarchical only)*	1 2 3 4 5	
Appropriate - Leadership links individuals to shared purpose	1 2 3 4 5	
Integrated – Leadership linked with all other aspects of the enterprise	1 2 3 4 5	

Notes / comments:

Active learning

Dimension	Score	Trend
Efficient - Appropriate theory provides ground for learning in practice	1 2 3 4 5	
Reliable - Feedback directs and indicates improvement *Also score high if feedback is positive / constructive; low if feedback is negative / destructive*	1 2 3 4 5	
Elegant - All personnel are involved in improving skills and workflows *Score high for interactive TQM / Quality Circles etc; low for Taylorist top-down imposition*	1 2 3 4 5	
Appropriate - Learning is linked to individual and shared purpose	1 2 3 4 5	
Integrated – Learning linked with all other aspects of the enterprise	1 2 3 4 5	

Notes / comments:

Narrative and dialogue

Dimension	Score	Trend
Efficient - Processes support openness and transparency *Score low for high levels of secrecy and control, unless explicitly required by purpose; also score low for intentional manipulation or misuse of stories (e.g. 'greenwash')*	1 2 3 4 5	
Reliable - Personal knowledge is recognised and supported *Score low if attempts are made to force all knowledge into the explicit 'objective' domain*	1 2 3 4 5	
Elegant - Stories, history and learnings arise from mutual 'conversation' *Score high for multi-way dialogue / feedback; low if communication is 'one-way' broadcast*	1 2 3 4 5	
Appropriate - Stories and history reflect personal and shared purpose *Score low if 'anti-stories' indicate high levels of cynicism and disconnect; also score low if stories indicate high levels of 'us and them' antagonism / power-against*	1 2 3 4 5	
Integrated – Personal knowledge linked with all other aspects of the enterprise	1 2 3 4 5	

Notes / comments:

Sense-making and foresight

Dimension	Score	Trend
Efficient - Strategy leverages and balances past, present and future *Score low if strategy is derived from only one or two of these (e.g. no anchor in past)*	1 2 3 4 5	
Reliable - Strategy allows for emergence and uncertainty *Score low for traditional 'same as last plus 10%' strategic planning unless appropriate*	1 2 3 4 5	
Elegant - All stakeholders are involved in development of strategy *Score high for broad engagement; low for 'insider-only' or 'top-down' development*	1 2 3 4 5	
Appropriate - Strategy reflects personal and shared purpose *Score low if collective strategy reflects only one group's purpose (e.g. shareholders)*	1 2 3 4 5	
Integrated – Strategy and foresight linked with all other aspects of the enterprise	1 2 3 4 5	

Notes / comments:

Responsibility and empowerment

Dimension	Score	Trend
Efficient - Type of power applied is appropriate to each task *Score low if type is not appropriate (e.g. 'analysis paralysis' as over-reliance on mental)*	1 2 3 4 5	
Reliable - Each person has a sense of personal ownership of their tasks *Score high for self-organisation; low for command-and-control imposition of tasks*	1 2 3 4 5	
Elegant - Relations are based on mutual understanding and respect *Score low if relationships are based on fear or domination*	1 2 3 4 5	
Appropriate - Tasks support both personal and shared purpose *Score low for imbalanced support, or if support for any purpose is low*	1 2 3 4 5	
Integrated – Responsibility and authority linked with all other aspects of the enterprise	1 2 3 4 5	

Notes / comments:

Integration - bringing it all together

Dimension	Score	Trend
Efficient - Business models support overall integration *Score high for 'living organisation' etc; low for 'business as machine for making money'; also score low if support for generalists is poor*	1 2 3 4 5	
Reliable - Context supports system-wide feedback and reflection *Score high for meditation or large-group interventions etc; low for 'business as usual'*	1 2 3 4 5	
Elegant - Integration supports diversity of skills, background, experience *Score high for diversity and/or appropriate use of uniformity; low for imposed uniformity*	1 2 3 4 5	
Appropriate - Context is effective and 'on purpose' *Score low for over-focus on local efficiency at the expense of overall effectiveness*	1 2 3 4 5	
Integrated - Quality and consistency of integration in the overall context	1 2 3 4 5	

Notes / comments:

APPENDIX A: GLOSSARY

This glossary describes specific meanings of terms used in SEMPER. Cross-references between terms are shown in *italic* text.

active learning	systematic process of reflection on action, to develop skills and competencies; examples include action-learning/action-research, Quality Circles, debriefing and task self-assessment; link-theme between *mental dimension* and *physical dimension*
appropriate	matching the intended overall purpose; a *REAL / LEARN* effectiveness-assessment theme associated with the *spiritual dimension* of the context
aspirational dimension	see *spiritual dimension*
behavioural dimension	see *physical dimension*
business-as-usual	shorthand term for a common *paradigm* of business and business-management characterised by a command-and-control model, *win/lose* transactions, short-term thinking, narrow focus, an over-emphasis on *efficiency* at the expense of overall *effectiveness*, and lack of awareness of the *performance paradox*
chaos	domain of inherent uncertainty and unpredictability; in the business context, may be partially concealed in demographics and other aggregates, but at the individual level all real-world transactions involve some chaos and *complexity*; also useful when invoked intentionally in creativity, in *narrative* and *dialogue*, and in *foresight* techniques such as *scenario* construction
complexity	domain of *emergent* properties and non-linear relationships between factors; unlike chaos, which is inherently uncertain, may often create an illusion of predictability, especially where linear analysis is applied within a short-term, narrow set of assumptions
conceptual dimension	see *mental dimension*

dialogue	process of *emergent* conversation in which awareness and knowledge are created between the people involved; link-theme between *mental dimension* and *emotional dimension*
effective	'on purpose', producing the intended overall result with an *optimised* balance over the whole context; requires broad generalist awareness of the whole, rather than the narrow focus required to create local efficiency, hence often contrasted with *efficient*
efficient	'doing more with less', creating the maximum result with the minimum use or waste of resources in a specific activity or context; improved incrementally through *active learning* and related techniques; major improvements usually require a change in *paradigm*; a *REAL / LEARN* effectiveness-assessment theme associated with the *mental dimension* of the context
elegant	human dimensions of *effectiveness*, such as feelings, emotions and ergonomics, expressed in issues such as usability, simplicity and personal preference; a *REAL / LEARN* effectiveness-assessment theme associated with the *emotional dimension* of the context
emergence	context within which cause-effect patterns can be identified only retrospectively, and in which analytic techniques are usually unreliable and misleading
emotional dimension	relational and emotional aspects of the work context: feelings and *values*, internal relationships and interpersonal transactions, relationships with external stakeholders; also assets such as reputation and trust; see also *vision, value; leadership; narrative, dialogue*
empowerment	the process and practice of deriving *power* from within the self, or assisting others through *power-with*; link-theme between *spiritual dimension* and *physical dimension*
foresight	the discipline of developing a forward view in time; link-theme between *spiritual dimension* and *mental dimension*; see also *sense-making; strategy, scenario*
goal	a specific objective to be achieved by or before a specified point in time; contrasted with *mission, purpose* and *vision*
integration	contextual awareness of all the interactions between the *physical, mental, emotional* and *spiritual* dimensions of work and the workspace, and the active process of linking them together into a unified whole

leadership	mentoring, coaching, example and other processes for guidance of Self and Other in action; link-theme between *physical dimension* and *emotional dimension*
lose/win	dysfunctional *power*-transaction (*power-against*) in which one attempts to help the Other win by making Self lose
mental dimension	mental and conceptual aspects of work and the workspace: beliefs, attitudes, knowledge, procedures and process specifications; also knowledge-assets and intellectual capital
mental model	chosen set of beliefs and method to interpret a given context; usually underpinned by a less-conscious *paradigm* or *worldview*
mission	a desired state to be achieved, usually within a specified timeframe, and to be maintained indefinitely thereafter; contrasted with *goal*, *purpose* and *vision*
narrative	personalised and often emotive expression or interpretation of knowledge, as history, anecdote or story; link-theme between *mental dimension* and *emotional dimension*
optimisation	process of *integration* in which *efficiency* in different areas is traded-off and balanced for maximum *effectiveness* over the whole; in any complex or layered context, the process relies extensively on the *REAL / LEARN* themes (*efficient, reliable, elegant, appropriate, integrated*) to identify the energies and resources to be balanced, and on the R^5 principles (*recursion, rotation, reflexion, reciprocation, resonance*) to identify balances and trade-offs between layers and sub-contexts such as departments, business processes and business units
paradigm	coherent set of beliefs about cause-effect relationships within a given class of context
performance paradox	an *effectiveness* paradox in which a desired result is achieved by paying attention to everything except the desired result; arises where that result depends on *emergent* properties derived from the *optimisation* of many factors in *complex* non-linear relationships – for example, a *business-as-usual* over-focus on financial results produces weaker financial performance than a focus on *integration* issues such as customer service and employee satisfaction
physical dimension	physical aspects of work and the workspace: skills, competencies, physical processes, behaviours, actions; also tangible assets and work-environment

power	the ability to do work; in human terms, includes the ability to work, play, relate, learn, as an expression of personal choice, responsibility and purpose, and with awareness and respect of shared purpose; exists only within the Self; see also *power-with, power-against*
power-against	collective *win/lose* or *lose/win* process in which *power* is mistakenly believed to be transferred between Self and Other; contrasted with *power-with*
power-with	collective *win/win* process to assist Self and/or Other to access personal *power*; contrasted with *power-against*
principle	a conceptual commitment or model, the mental-dimension equivalent of *value*
purpose	a declared role within the 'world' described by a *vision*; contrasted with *goal, mission* and *vision*
R⁵	collective term for five complexity-science principles used with the *tetradian*, namely *recursion, rotation, reflexion, reciprocation* and *resonance*.
REAL/ LEARN	acronym for four keywords to evaluate effectiveness: *reliable, efficient, appropriate, elegant*; the LEARN acronym includes *integration* in the evaluation-set
reciprocation	overall balance in transactions, especially *power-transactions*; reciprocal balance between entities may not be direct or immediate, and in many cases balance may only be achieved over time at a system-wide level, with energy-transfers occurring between *physical, mental, emotional* and/or *spiritual* dimensions; an *R⁵* principle for assessment of *effectiveness* and relevance
recursion	patterns of relationship or interaction repeat or are 'self-similar' at different scales; permits simplification of otherwise complex processes; an *R⁵* principle for assessment of *effectiveness* and relevance
reflexion	corollary of *recursion*, in that the whole, or aspects of the whole, can be identified within the attributes and transactions of any part at any scale; an *R⁵* principle for assessment of *effectiveness* and relevance
relational dimension	see *emotional dimension*
reliable	high degree of certainty and predictability for a desired outcome; a *REAL/LEARN* effectiveness-assessment theme associated with the *physical dimension* of the context

resonance	impacts of positive- or negative-feedback (increasing or damping) in a system; permits simplification of otherwise complex processes; an R^5 principle for assessment of *effectiveness* and relevance
responsibility	literally 'response-ability', the ability to choose and act upon appropriate responses according to context, as an expression of personal *power*; link-theme between *spiritual dimension* and *physical dimension*
rotation	systematic process of assessing a context from multiple perspectives; an R^5 principle for assessment of *effectiveness* and relevance
scenario	an imagined future context, developed for the purpose of understanding both the present context and options for action in the future context; a *foresight* technique
self-propagation	aspect of *integration* in which a meme – an idea, a practice, a way of relating – spreads throughout an enterprise, requiring little or no effort or intervention beyond the initial 'seeding'; contrasted with the more typical 'command-and-control' *tactics* of *business-as-usual*, which require constant effort and intervention to impose a meme throughout the enterprise
SEMPER	acronym for *Spiritual, Emotional, Mental, Physical, Effectiveness (REAL / LEARN)*, Relevance (R^5); alternatively, acronym for 'System Effectiveness Map for Process Evaluation and Review'; also the Latin word for 'always'
sense-making	the process of creating *mental models* to provide a conceptual framework for understanding ambiguity, *emergence* and uncertainty; link-theme between *spiritual dimension* and *mental dimension*; see also *foresight*
spiritual dimension	aspirational and intentional aspects of work and the workplace, expressed in collective and individual identity and purpose, and in issues such as ethics, values and codes of conduct; also commitment-assets and spiritual capital such as organisational morale, health and fitness; see also *vision, value; sense-making, foresight; empowerment, responsibility*

'start anywhere' principle	corollary of *self-propagation*, in that 'seeding' for *integration* may start from any aspect of the enterprise – usually away from nominal 'problems' – allowing *emergence* to indicate 'winners' for further propagation; contrasts with conventional interventions which attempt to tackle 'problem'-issues head-on, often further inflaming the problem, or transferring the problem elsewhere within the organisation
strategy	'big picture' view of a plan of action, usually incorporating *vision, mission* and *goal*; contrasted with *tactics* required to execute the plan
tactics	detailed step-by-step activities to execute a *strategy*, or some segment of an overall strategy
tetradian (*alt.* tetradion)	depiction of the *physical, mental, emotional* and *spiritual* dimensions as four axes in a tetrahedral relationship, usually also showing the respective link-themes as the edges between the vertices of the tetrahedron
value	an emotional commitment; link-theme between *spiritual dimension* and *emotional dimension*
vision	description of a desired 'world', always far greater than any individual or organisation; described in the present tense, yet is never 'achieved'; contrasted with *goal, mission* and *purpose*; link-theme between *spiritual dimension* and *emotional dimension*
win/lose	dysfunctional *power*-transaction (*power-against*) in which one Self attempts to win by forcing the Other to lose
win/win	functional *power*-transaction in which both Self and Other achieve part or all of their objectives for the transaction; contrasted with the dysfunctional 'lose/lose' transactions *win/lose* and *lose/win*
worldview	largely unconscious but generally coherent set of beliefs about how the world operates; at the level of day-to-day practice, approximately synonymous with *paradigm*

APPENDIX B: SOURCES AND RESOURCES

This section lists sources for books, white-papers and other on-line resources mentioned in the text.

Online SEMPER metrics: see 🕸 www.sempermetrics.com

Balanced Scorecard: see 🕸 www.balancedscorecard.org

Belbin Team Roles: see 🕸 www.belbin.com

Business process re-engineering: see 📖 Michael Hammer and James Champy, *Reengineering the Corporation: A Manifesto for Business Revolution* (HarperBusiness, 1993)

Cluetrain Manifesto: see 🕸 www.cluetrain.com and 📖 Rick Levine, Christopher Locke, Doc Searls, and David Weinberger, *The Cluetrain Manifesto: The End of Business As Usual* (Perseus Books, 2000)

Communities of practice: see 📖 Etienne Wenger, Richard McDermott and William Snyder, *Cultivating Communities of Practice: A Guide to Managing Knowledge* (Harvard Business School Press, 2002)

Cynefin, complexity and David Snowden: see 🕸 www.cognitive-edge.com and summary at 🕸 en.wikipedia.org/wiki/Cynefin

Demand innovation: see 📖 Adrian Slywotzky, Richard Wise and Karl Weber, *How to Grow When Markets Don't: Discovering the New Drivers of Growth* (Warner Books, 2003)

Deming and quality-management: see 📖 W Edwards Deming, *Out of the Crisis*, 2nd edition (Cambridge University Press; 1988)

Dialogue process: see 📖 David Bohm, *On Dialogue* (Routledge; 1996)

Emotional intelligence: see 📖 Daniel Goleman, *Emotional Intelligence* (Bantam USA, 1997)

Futures in the business context: see 📖 Gary Hamel and C.K. Prahalad, *Competing for the Future* (Harvard Business School Press, 1996), and Sohail Inayatullah, 'Causal Layered Analysis' 🕸 www.metafuture.org/Articles/CausalLayeredAnalysis.htm

Group Dynamics: see summary at 🕸 en.wikipedia.org/Group_Dynamics

Integrated Performance Support Systems: see summary at
🕸 en.wikipedia.org/wiki/Electronic_performance_support_systems

Knowledge-management processes: see, for example, 📖 Chris
Collison and Geoff Parcell, *Learning to Fly: Practical Lessons from
one of the World's Leading Knowledge Companies* (Capstone, 2001)

Large group interventions (including Open Space and Future
Search): see *Leith's Guide to Large Group Intervention Methods* at
🕸 (PDF) www.beratungspool.ch/dossiers/grossgruppen/guide.pdf

Leadership: see, for example, 📖 Stephen R. Covey, *Principle-
centered Leadership* (Simon & Schuster, 1999)

'Living enterprise' metaphor: see 📖 Arie de Geus, *The Living
Company* (Harvard Business School Press, 1997) and 📖 Charles
Handy, *Beyond Certainty: The Changing Worlds of Organizations*
(Harvard Business School Press, 1998); also the Royal Society of
Arts 'Centre for Tomorrow's Company', at
🕸 www.tomorrowscompany.com

Narrative knowledge: see, for example, 🕸 www.anecdote.com.au

Open Space: see 🕸 www.openspaceworld.org and summary at
🕸 en.wikipedia.org/wiki/Open_Space_Technology

Ricardo Semler and Semco: see Ricardo Semler, 📖 *Maverick: The
Success Story Behind the World's Most Unusual Workplace* (Arrow
Books, 1994) and 📖 *The Seven-Day Weekend: A Better Way to
Work in the 21st Century* (Century, 2004)

Scenarios and strategy: see 📖 Peter Schwartz, *The Art of the Long
View: Scenario Planning - Protecting Your Company Against an
Uncertain Future* (Random House Business, 1992) and 📖 Kees
van der Heijden, *Scenarios: The Art of Strategic Conversation*, 2nd
edition (John Wiley & Sons, 2004)

Scientific management and Taylorism: see 📖 Frederick Taylor,
Principles of Scientific Management (Dover reprint, 1998; original
publication 1911); also summary at
🕸 en.wikipedia.org/wiki/Scientific_management

Seven Habits: see 📖 Stephen R. Covey, *Seven Habits of Highly
Effective People* (Simon & Schuster; 1999)

Six Hats decision-making technique: see 📖 Edward de Bono, *Six
Thinking Hats* (Viking, 1986)

'Soul' in the business context: see 📖 Richard Barrett, *Liberating the
Corporate Soul: Building a Visionary Organization* (Butterworth-
Heinemann, 1998)

Spiritual Intelligence: see 📖 Danah Zohar and Ian Marshall, *Spiritual Intelligence: The Ultimate Intelligence* (Bloomsbury Paperbacks, 2001)

Systems thinking: see Peter Sengé et al., 📖 *The Fifth Discipline: The Art and Practice of the Learning Organization* (Transworld, 1990), 📖 *The Fifth Discipline Fieldbook: Strategies for Building a Learning Organization* (Nicholas Brealey Publishing, 1994) and 📖 *The Dance of Change: The Challenges of Sustaining Momentum in Learning Organizations* (Nicholas Brealey Publishing, 1999)

Values in the workplace: see 🖥 www.valuesatwork.org and 📖 Michael Henderson and Dougal Thompson, *Values At Work: the invisible threads between people, performance and profit*, HarperBusiness (2003).

Viable Systems: see 📖 Stafford Beer, *The Brain of the Firm*, 2nd edition (John Wiley & Sons; 1994; original publication 1972) and 📖 Raúl Espejo and Roger Harnden (eds), *The Viable System Model: Interpretations and Applications of Stafford Beer's VSM* (John Wiley & Sons, 1989); also summary at 🖥 en.wikipedia.org/wiki/Viable_System_Model

Viral marketing: see 📖 Seth Godin, *Unleashing the Ideavirus: Stop Marketing at People! Turn Your Ideas Into Epidemics by Helping Your Customers Do the Marketing for You* (Hyperion Books, 2001); and 📖 Christopher Locke, *Gonzo Marketing: Winning Through Worst Practices* (Perseus Publishing, 2001)

Gerry Weinberg: see, for example, 📖 Gerald M Weinberg, *The Secrets of Consulting* (Dorset House, 1985)

Whole-of-enterprise architecture: see 📖 Tom Graves, *Real Enterprise Architecture: beyond IT to the whole enterprise* (Tetradian Books, 2008)

World Café: see 📖 Juanita Brown, David Isaacs et al., *The World Cafe: Shaping Our Futures Through Conversations That Matter* (Berrett-Koehler, 2005)

John Zachman and the Zachman Framework for enterprise architecture: see 🖥 www.zifa.com

www.ingramcontent.com/pod-product-compliance
Lightning Source LLC
Chambersburg PA
CBHW021602210326
41599CB00010B/562